DUTCH SOCCER DRILLS

DRILLS

Vol. 4

REEDSWAIN
PUBLISHING

**Library of Congress
Cataloging - in - Publication Data**

Dutch Soccer Drills
Volume 4

ISBN No. 1-59164-056-3
Lib. of Congress Catalog No. 96-41894
© 2003

Editing
Bryan R. Beaver

Printed by
DATA REPRODUCTIONS
Auburn, Michigan

Reedswain Publishing
612 Pughtown Road
Spring City, PA 19475
800.331.5191
www.reedswain.com
info@reedswain.com

CONTENTS

Chapter One

DRIBBLING
1-9

DRIBBLING

OBJECTIVE:
◆ To learn how to dribble into space while under pressure from an opponent

ORGANIZATION:
◆ The attackers try to dribble through as many goals as possible in a given time
◆ The defenders try to prevent this
◆ Who can dribble through 5 goals in the fastest time?

INSTRUCTIONS:
◆ Dribble with the ball close to your feet and change direction frequently
◆ Shield the ball with your body
◆ Look over the ball so that you see where your teammates and opponents are
◆ Dribble into space, covering ground quickly with the ball
◆ Feint to the right and left
◆ After feinting, pass, shoot or accelerate
◆ Feint with your body or by suddenly stopping and pretending to move in another direction, or by pretending that you are going to shoot or pass

OBJECTIVE:
* To learn how to dribble into space
* To learn how to react quickly to a teammate

ORGANIZATION:
* Pairs of players dribble around freely. Each pair carries out a given task.
* The second player in each pair follows the first one at a distance of 6 feet.
* The players swap places when a sign is given.

INSTRUCTIONS:
* Dribble with the ball close to your feet and change direction frequently
* Shield the ball with your body
* Look over the ball, so that you see where your teammates and opponents are
* Dribble into space, covering ground quickly with the ball
* Feint to the right and left
* After feinting, pass, shoot or accelerate
* Feint with your body or by suddenly stopping and pretending to move in another direction, or by pretending that you are going to shoot or pass

DRIBBLING 3

OBJECTIVE:
* To improve changes of direction and turns

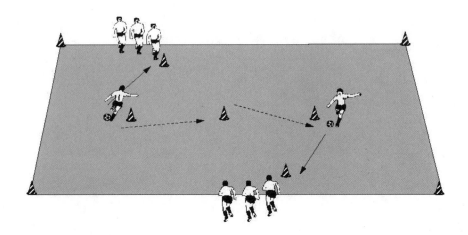

ORGANIZATION:
* Field measuring 20 x 20 yards
* 3 cones in a line
* 2 start cones at a distance of 10 yards from this line
* 8 to 10 players
* 8 to 10 balls

INSTRUCTIONS:
* Practice for about 10 minutes
* Change of direction using the inside of the foot; practice with the right and the left foot
* Change of direction using the outside of the foot; practice with the right and the left foot
* Step over the ball to the right and left
* After each change of direction, pass the ball, using the inside of the foot, to the next player.
* 4 or 5 players at each start cone; rest period of 30 to 45 seconds for each player

OBJECTIVE:
- To improve feinting and taking the ball past an opponent

ORGANIZATION:
- Space the cones about 8 yards apart
- 1 player must defend the line between the cones. The attackers take turns trying to dribble the ball past the defender between the cones.
- After crossing the line, the attacker stays in this half until it is his turn again.
- If the defender succeeds in winning the ball, the attacker and the defender swap roles.

INSTRUCTIONS:
- Feint before you get too close to the defender
- Use your body when you feint
- Pass the defender on the right and on the left and use a variety of feints
- Do not approach the defender too fast
- Accelerate after feinting or passing the defender.

DRIBBLING

OBJECTIVE:
* To improve individual actions: dribbling, passing, shooting and defending

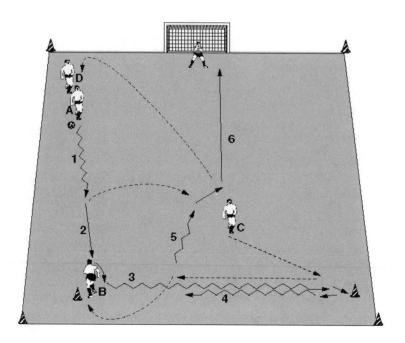

ORGANIZATION:
* Field measuring 20 x 30 yards
* 4 to 6 players and 1 goalkeeper
* 6 balls

INSTRUCTIONS:
* Player A dribbles and passes the ball to B
* Player B dribbles to the other cone and back
* Player C pressures player B, but not 100 percent
* 1v1
* Player A goes to player C's position, player C goes to player B's position, and player B goes to the start position
* After 30 seconds player D starts the sequence anew

OBJECTIVE:
• To improve individual actions: dribbling, passing, shooting and defending

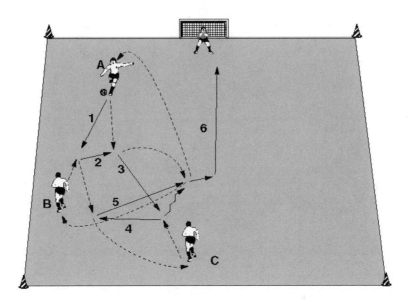

ORGANIZATION:
• Field measuring 20 x 30 yards
• 6 to 8 players and 1 goalkeeper
• 6 balls

INSTRUCTIONS:
• Player A passes to the incoming player B
• Player B passes back to player A (1 touch)
• Player A passes to the incoming player C
• Player C passes to the incoming player B
• Player B passes back to player C (1 touch), who then tries to dribble the ball past player A
• Player C goes to player A's position, player A goes to player B's position, and player B goes to player C's position

DRIBBLING

7

OBJECTIVE:
* To improve individual actions: dribbling, passing, shooting and defending

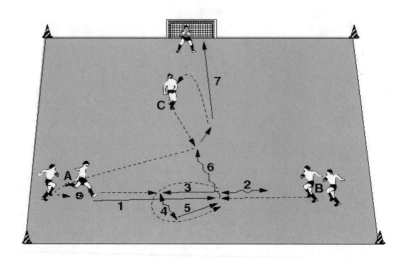

ORGANIZATION:
* Field measuring 20 x 30 yards
* 3 to 6 players and 1 goalkeeper
* 6 balls
* Duration: 20 minutes

INSTRUCTIONS:
* Player A passes to the incoming player B
* Player B feints twice and passes back to the incoming player A
* Player B runs round player A
* Player A feints twice and passes back to the incoming player B
* Player C pressures player B, who feints and dribbles the ball past player C and then shoots at the goal
* Player A goes to player B's position, player C goes to player A's position, and player B goes to player C's position and starts the sequence again

OBJECTIVE:
* To improve individual actions: dribbling, passing, shooting and defending

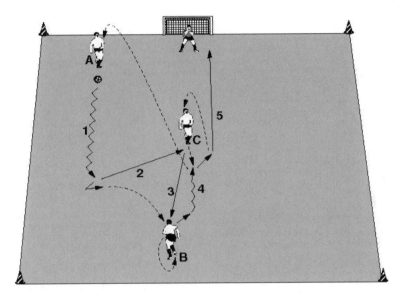

ORGANIZATION:
* Field measuring 20 x 20 yards
* 3 to 6 players and 1 goalkeeper
* 4 balls
* Duration: 20 minutes

INSTRUCTIONS:
* Player A dribbles to the middle and feints
* Player A then passes to player C
* Player C passes to player B
* Player A immediately pressures player B
* Player B tries to dribble the ball past player A
* After taking the ball past player A, player B tries to dribble it past player C
* Player B shoots at goal
* Player A goes to player B's position, player B goes to player C's position, and player C goes to player A's starting position

DRIBBLING

OBJECTIVE:
* To improve individual actions: dribbling, passing, shooting and defending

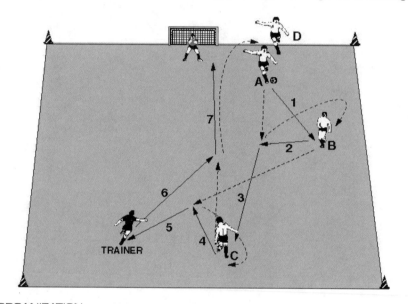

ORGANIZATION:
* Field measuring 20 x 30 yards
* 5 or 6 players and 1 goalkeeper
* 6 balls

INSTRUCTIONS:
* Player A passes to player B
* Player B passes back to the incoming player A
* Player A passes to player C
* Player C passes to the incoming player B
* Player B passes to the coach
* The coach passes into the path of the incoming player C, who shoots at goal
* Player D starts the sequence again
* Players A takes player B's position and player B takes player C's position
* Player C has a 30-second break

VARIATION
* With one defender in front of the goal and a 1v1 before shooting

Chapter Two

PASSING
10-55

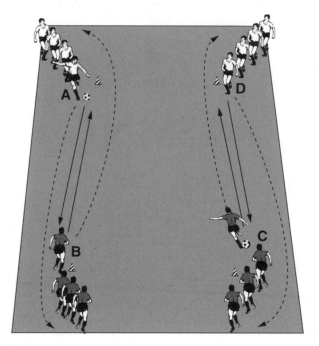

PASSING

OBJECTIVE:
* To improve passing and kicking technique

ORGANIZATION:
* Field measuring 15 x 15 yards
* 4 players at each cone
* The ball is passed at speed from player A to player B, who passes it back to player A
* The ball is passed at speed from player C to player D, who passes it back to player C
* The players run forward after passing and join the back of the line at the opposite cone

INSTRUCTIONS:
* Concentrate on passing
* Pass to the receiving player's stronger foot, or pass the ball directly into the path of the receiving player
* Face the ball
* Feint to make a run before receiving the ball
* Keep moving

PASSING

OBJECTIVE:
* To improve passing and kicking technique

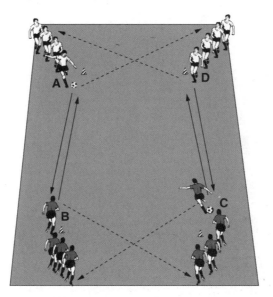

ORGANIZATION:
* Field measuring 15 x 15 yards
* 4 players at each cone
* The ball is passed at speed from player A to player B, who passes it back to player A
* The ball is passed at speed from player C to player D, who passes it back to player C
* After passing the ball, the player runs to the side
* Player A joins group D after passing the ball
* Player B joins group C after passing the ball
* Player C joins group B after passing the ball
* Player D joins group A after passing the ball

INSTRUCTIONS:
* Concentrate on passing
* Pass to the receiving player's stronger foot, or pass the ball directly into the path of the receiving player
* Face the ball
* Feint to make a run before receiving the ball
* Keep moving

PASSING

OBJECTIVE:
* To improve passing and kicking technique

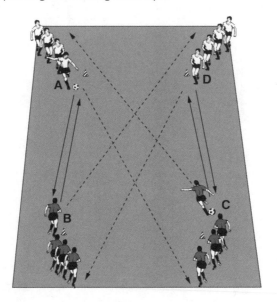

ORGANIZATION:
* Field measuring 15 x 15 yards
* 4 players at each cone
* The ball is passed at speed from player A to player B, who passes it back to player A
* The ball is passed at speed from player C to player D, who passes it back to player C
* After passing the ball, the player runs diagonally forward
* Player A joins group C after passing the ball
* Player B joins group D after passing the ball
* Player C joins group A after passing the ball
* Player D joins group B after passing the ball

INSTRUCTIONS:
* Concentrate on passing
* Pass to the receiving player's stronger foot, or pass the ball directly into the path of the receiving player
* Face the ball
* Feint to make a run before receiving the ball
* Keep moving

PASSING

OBJECTIVE:
* To improve passing and kicking technique

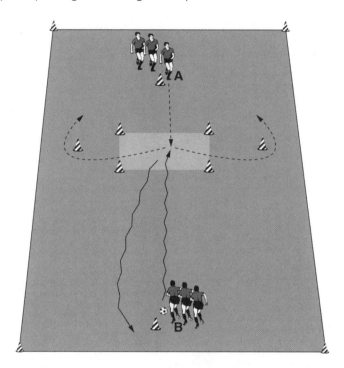

ORGANIZATION:
* Player B dribbles the ball towards the approaching player A
* Player A takes over the ball and joins group B
* Player B sprints as fast as he can to the right or left and then joins group A
* The players sprint 3 times to the right and 3 times to the left

INSTRUCTIONS:
* Concentrate on passing
* Pass to the receiving player's stronger foot, or pass the ball directly into the path of the receiving player
* Face the ball
* Feint to make a run before receiving the ball
* Keep moving

OBJECTIVE:
• To improve passing and kicking technique

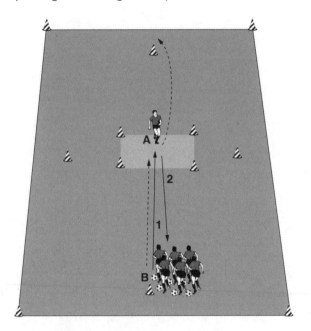

ORGANIZATION:
• The first player in group B passes to player A
• Player A plays the ball back (1 touch) to the next player in group B
• Player A turns and sprints to the cone
• The first player in group B takes over the position of player A
• The next player in group B passes to the new player A
• The new player A plays the ball back (1 touch) to the next player in group B
• The new player A turns and sprints to the cone
• This sequence is repeated 6 times

INSTRUCTIONS:
• Concentrate on passing
• Pass to the receiving player's stronger foot, or pass the ball directly into the path of the receiving player
• Face the ball
• Feint to make a run before receiving the ball
• Keep moving

PASSING

OBJECTIVE:

• To improve passing and kicking technique

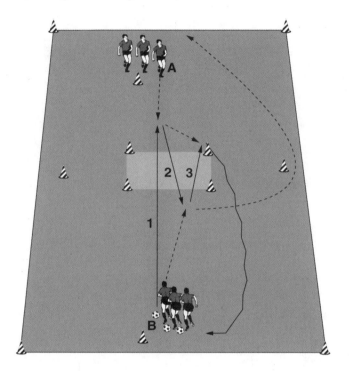

ORGANIZATION:

• Player B plays the ball to the approaching player A
• Player A plays the ball back (1 touch) to the approaching player B
• Player B plays the ball back (1 touch) to the approaching player A
• Player B sprints round the cone and joins group A
• Player A dribbles the ball to group B
• The sequence is repeated until 3 sprints have been carried out to the right and 3 to the left

INSTRUCTIONS:

• Concentrate on passing
• Pass to the receiving player's stronger foot, or pass the ball directly into the path of the receiving player
• Face the ball
• Keep moving

OBJECTIVE:
* To improve passing and kicking technique

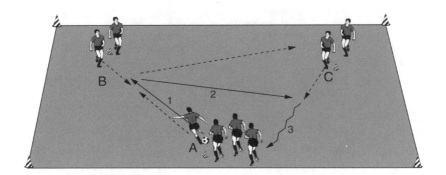

ORGANIZATION:
* Player A passes the ball firmly to the left foot of player B
* Player B controls the ball and passes it firmly into the path of player C
* Player A takes over the position of player B and player B takes over the position of player C
* Repeat the sequence a few times, then repeat it in the other direction (play the ball to the other foot)

INSTRUCTIONS:
* Concentrate on passing
* Pass to the receiving player's stronger foot, or pass the ball directly into the path of the receiving player
* Face the ball
* Feint to make a run before receiving the ball
* Keep moving

OBJECTIVE:
* To improve passing and kicking technique

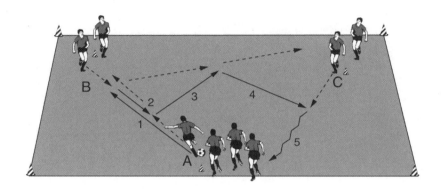

ORGANIZATION:
* Player A passes the ball firmly to player B
* Player B plays the ball back to player A (1 touch), who plays it into the path of player B
* Player B plays the ball firmly into the path of player C
* Player A takes over the position of player B, player B takes over the position of player C, and player C takes over the position of player A
* Repeat the sequence a few times, then repeat it in the other direction (play the ball to the other foot)

INSTRUCTIONS:
* Concentrate on passing
* Pass to the receiving player's stronger foot, or pass the ball directly into the path of the receiving player
* Face the ball
* Feint to make a run before receiving the ball
* Keep moving

OBJECTIVE:
• To improve passing and kicking technique

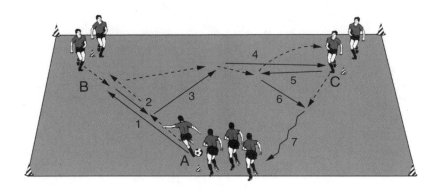

ORGANIZATION:
• Player A passes the ball firmly to player B
• Player B plays the ball back to player A (1 touch), who plays it into the path of player B
• Player B passes the ball firmly to player C, who plays a 1-2 combination with player B
• Repeat the sequence a few times, then repeat it in the other direction

INSTRUCTIONS:
• Concentrate on passing
• Pass to the receiving player's stronger foot, or pass the ball directly into the path of the receiving player
• Face the ball
• Feint to make a run before receiving the ball
• Keep moving

PASSING

OBJECTIVE:
* To improve controlling a pass and running with the ball using the right and the left foot

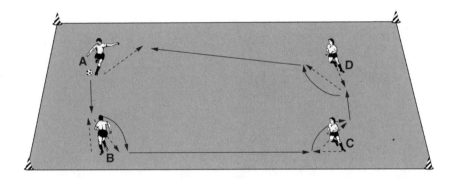

ORGANIZATION:
* Player A passes to player B, who controls the ball and takes it to the right in 1 movement
* Player B passes to player C, etc.
* The players remain in the same area
* The players pass the ball in the other direction, so that they have to turn to the left
* The players should stand about 12 yards apart at the sides

INSTRUCTIONS:
* Feint before taking the ball into space to the right or left.
* Always keep the ball close to your foot
* Use both the inside and outside of the foot
* Play the ball behind your standing leg
* Use both the left and the right foot
* After moving to the right or left, look up to see where the other players are positioned
* 4 to 8 players can take part
* If 6 or more players are involved, the players should continue running to the next position after playing the ball, so that they spend less time standing still

OBJECTIVE:
* To improve passing and kicking technique

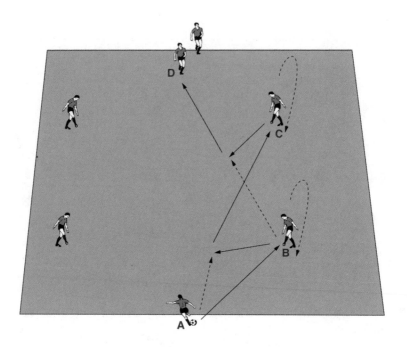

ORGANIZATION:
* The ball should always be passed with the first touch
* The pass should be made with the inside of the foot after feinting to make a run
* Player A passes to player B, who uses his right foot to play the ball back into the path of player A, who uses his left foot to pass to player C, who uses his right foot to play the ball into the path of player B
* The sequence is repeated in the opposite direction
* Place a defender beside player B
* Instead of playing the 1-2 combination, player B turns and passes to player C

INSTRUCTIONS:
* Keep your ankle stretched when passing the ball
* Use your arms to maintain balance

PASSING

OBJECTIVE:
* To improve long-passing with the instep, using the right and the left foot

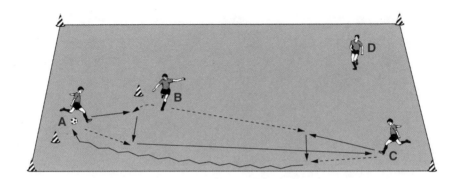

ORGANIZATION:
* Player A plays the ball into the path of player B
* Player B passes back to A and A strikes a long pass, using the instep, to player C
* Player C passes to the incoming player B, who plays the ball back to player C
* Player C takes over the position of player A, player A takes over the position of player B, and player B takes over the position of player C
* The sequence is repeated, but this time the long pass is made to player D
* Depending on the players' ages, the long pass is made over a distance of 25 to 50 yards

INSTRUCTIONS:
* Keep your foot pointing down when striking the long pass
* Aim to strike the ball just under the center
* Place the supporting foot sufficiently far from the ball to enable the ball to be struck with the foot pointing down
* Keep your upper body vertical and use the arms to maintain balance
* If there are more players, organize them into several groups
* Each group should have a minimum of 6 players

OBJECTIVE:
- To improve passing over a short distance

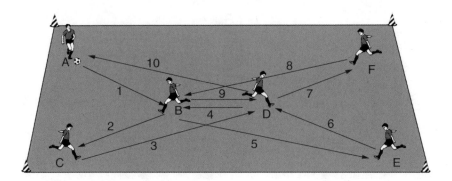

ORGANIZATION:
- Player A passes to player B
- Player B passes to player C
- Player C passes to player D, who passes to player B
- Player B passes to player E
- Player E passes to player D
- Player D passes to player F
- Player F passes to player B, who passes to player D
- Player D passes to player A

INSTRUCTIONS:
- Carry out this sequence over the left as well as the right side
- After 2 sequences the players push up one place
- This drill can also be carried out with 8 players

OBJECTIVE:

• To improve passing and kicking technique

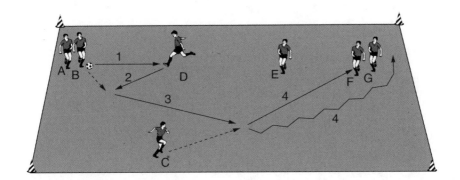

ORGANIZATION:

• Player B passes to player D
• Player D passes to the incoming player B
• Player B plays the ball into the path of player C
• Player C passes to player F or dribbles the ball until he is behind player G

INSTRUCTIONS:

• Start the sequence simultaneously on the other side
• Carry out the sequence to the left as well as the right
• The players push up to the following position

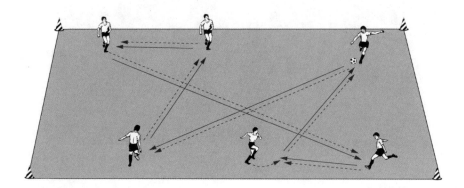

PASSING

OBJECTIVE:
* To improve passing with the side of the foot (right and left foot)
* To improve controlling a pass and running with the ball
* To improve movement after passing

ORGANIZATION:
* Field measuring 10 x 20 yards
* 4 to 6 players
* 1 ball
* Work to rest ratio: 1:1
* 5 series of 90 seconds, 8 series of 1 minute; total 10 to 16 minutes

INSTRUCTIONS:
* Passing technique
* The players must keep moving all the time
* Look at whether the players run on their toes
* If a player makes a mistake, explain this and ask him/her to repeat the action
* Introduce obstacles
* Make the area smaller or larger
* Switch players more quickly
* Increase the length of the drill period
* Check heartbeat during rest periods

OBJECTIVE:
* To improve passing and kicking technique

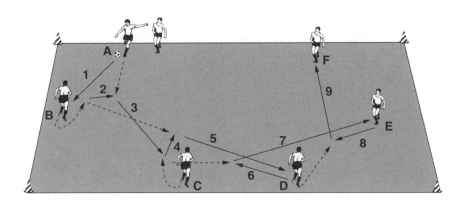

ORGANIZATION:
* Player A passes to player B
* Player B feints to make a run, then plays the ball into the path of the incoming player A
* Player A passes to player C
* Player C plays the ball into the path of the incoming player B
* Player B passes to player D
* Player D passes to the incoming player C
* Player C passes to player E
* Player E plays the ball into the path of the incoming player D, who passes to player F

INSTRUCTIONS:
* Concentrate on passing
* Pass to the receiving player's stronger foot, or pass the ball directly into the path of the receiving player
* Face the ball
* Feint to make a run before receiving the ball
* Keep moving

OBJECTIVE:
* To improve passing and kicking technique

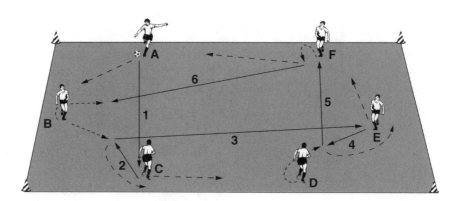

INSTRUCTIONS:
* This drill has no fixed pattern
* Each player must make choices about who to pass the ball to
* Sometimes a player misses out one position in the sequence from A to F
* The players are allowed to control the ball before passing
* The players must focus on how they pass the ball
* The players move continuously through the positions from A to F

NOTES:
* Look for the opportunity to play a long forward pass
* Create and recognize situations, run off the ball
* Concentrate on passing
* Play the ball to the receiving player's strongest foot or pass the ball directly into the path of the receiving player
* Face the ball
* Feint to make a run before receiving the ball
* Keep moving

PASSING

OBJECTIVE:
* To improve passing and kicking technique

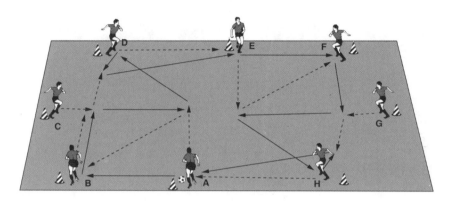

ORGANIZATION:
* Player A passes to player B
* Player B plays the ball to the incoming player C and continues running behind the ball
* Player C plays the ball to the incoming player A
* Player A plays the ball to player D
* Player D passes to the incoming player B
* Player B passes to player E
* Player E plays the ball to player F
* Player F plays the ball to the incoming player G
* Player G plays the ball to the incoming player E, who plays the ball to player H
* Player H plays the ball to the incoming player G, who plays the ball to the incoming player H

INSTRUCTIONS:
* Concentrate on passing
* Pass to the receiving player's stronger foot, or pass the ball directly into the path of the receiving player
* Face the ball
* Keep moving

PASSING

OBJECTIVE:
 * To improve passing and kicking technique

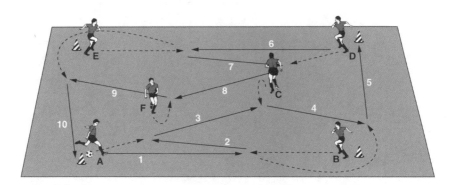

ORGANIZATION:
 * Player A passes to the incoming player B
 * Player B plays the ball back to player A, who is making a diagonal run
 * Player A plays the ball to the incoming player C, who feints to make a run
   before turning to receive the pass
 * Player C passes to the incoming player B
 * Player B plays the ball to player D
 * Player D passes to the incoming player E
 * Player E passes to the incoming player D
 * Player D passes to the incoming player F, who feints to make a run before
   turning to receive the pass
 * Player F passes to the incoming player E
 * Player E passes to player A

INSTRUCTIONS:
 * Concentrate on passing
 * Pass to the receiving player's stronger foot, or pass the ball directly into
   the path of the receiving player
 * Face the ball
 * Feint to make a run before receiving the ball
 * Keep moving

PASSING

OBJECTIVE:
* To improve passing and kicking technique

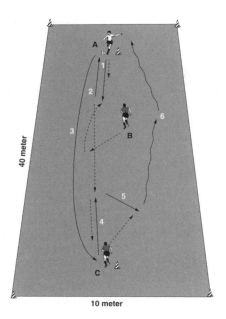

ORGANIZATION:
* Player B feints to make a run then turns back after 5 yards to receive a pass from player A
* Player B passes to player A
* Player A plays the ball to player C
* Player C plays a 1-2 combination with the incoming player B
* Player A goes to the position of player B
* Player B goes to the position of player C
* Player C dribbles the ball quickly to the position of player A

INSTRUCTIONS:
* Mark out a field measuring 40 x 10 yards with cones. If a pass is so inaccurate that the ball leaves the field, the whole group is punished:
* 10 press-ups for the first offense
* 15 press-ups for the second offense
* 2 50-yard sprints for the third offense
* 4 50-yard sprints for the fourth offense

OBJECTIVE:
* To improve passing and kicking technique

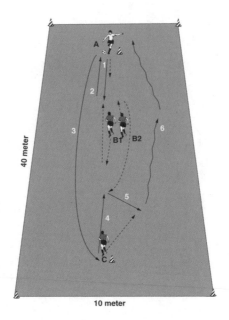

40 meter

10 meter

ORGANIZATION:
* Player B1 makes a run towards player C
* Player B2 makes a run toward the ball
* Player B1 calls for the ball from player A and plays a 1-2 combination with player A
* Player A hits a long, high, forward pass to player C
* Player B2 sprints toward player C to play a 1-2 combination
* Player B2 becomes player C, player B1 becomes player B2, player A becomes player B1 and player C becomes player A

INSTRUCTIONS:
* Series of 3 x 7 minutes. The ball must be played over the ground except for the high forward pass
* As well as developing passing and kicking technique, this drill teaches playing the ball to the third and even the fourth player

PASSING

OBJECTIVE:
* To improve passing and kicking technique

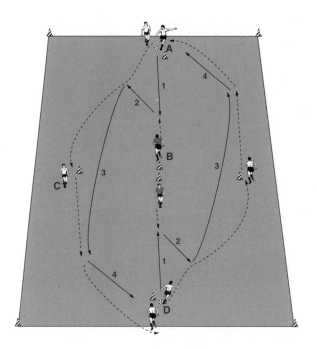

ORGANIZATION:
* Player A plays the ball to player B
* Player B passes back to player A
* Player A plays the ball to player C
* Player C plays the ball to player D
* Player A takes the place of player C
* Player C joins the line behind player D

INSTRUCTIONS:
* Try to pass the ball with the first touch
* Start with 1 ball, then introduce another, and if this goes well, introduce another 2
* Start on the right side, then switch to the left side after a while (depending on the number of players)

OBJECTIVE:
- To improve passing and kicking technique

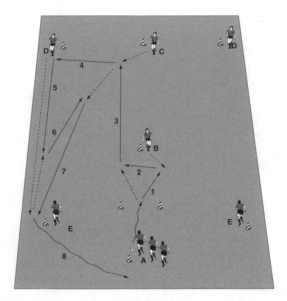

ORGANIZATION:
- Player A dribbles the ball between the cones and plays it to player B
- Player B returns the ball first time to the incoming player A
- Player A plays a long forward pass to player C
- Player C plays the ball to player D
- Player D plays the ball with his first touch to the incoming player E
- Player E plays the ball to the incoming player C
- Player C plays the ball into space for player D to run onto
- Player D joins the line behind player A
- Alternate between right and left
- The players push up one place after each sequence

INSTRUCTIONS:
- Concentrate on passing
- Pass to the receiving player's stronger foot, or pass the ball directly into the path of the receiving player
- Face the ball
- Feint to make a run before receiving the ball
- Keep moving

OBJECTIVE:
* To improve passing and kicking technique

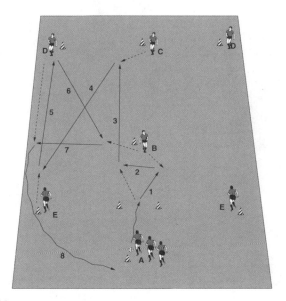

ORGANIZATION:
* Player A dribbles the ball between the cones and plays it to the incoming player B
* Player B plays the ball back to the incoming player A
* Player A plays a long forward pass to player C
* Player C skips player D and plays the ball to the incoming player E
* Player E plays the ball back to player D
* Player D plays a 1-2 combination with player B
* Players D and E swap places
* Player D joins the line behind player A
* Alternate between right and left
* The players push up one place after each sequence

INSTRUCTIONS:
* Concentrate on passing
* Pass to the receiving player's stronger foot, or pass the ball directly into the path of the receiving player
* Face the ball
* Feint to make a run before receiving the ball
* Keep moving

OBJECTIVE:
* To improve passing and kicking technique

ORGANIZATION:
* Player B feints to make a run, then turns to receive the ball
* Player A passes to player B
* Player B passes back to player A, who plays a long, low pass to player C
* Player D feints to run toward the ball before turning and calling for a forward pass
* Player D runs onto the ball and runs with it at speed, joining the group of players with the balls

INSTRUCTIONS:
* Keep your ankle stretched when passing the ball
* Keep your upper body vertical and use your arms for balance

PASSING

OBJECTIVE
• To improve passing and kicking technique

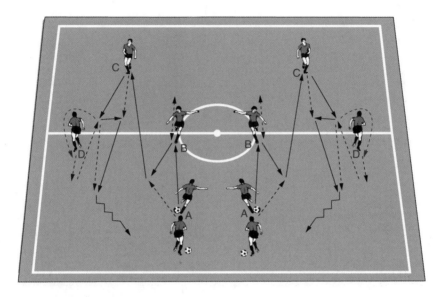

ORGANIZATION:
• Player B feints to make a run, then turns to receive the ball
• Player A passes to player B
• Player B passes back to player A, who plays a long, low pass to player C
• Player C passes to the incoming player D
• Player D passes back to player C, turns and sprints into space
• Player C passes into the path of player D, who runs onto the ball and runs with it at speed, joining the group of players with the balls

INSTRUCTIONS:
• Keep your ankle stretched when passing the ball
• Keep your upper body vertical and use your arms for balance

OBJECTIVE:
* To improve passing and kicking technique

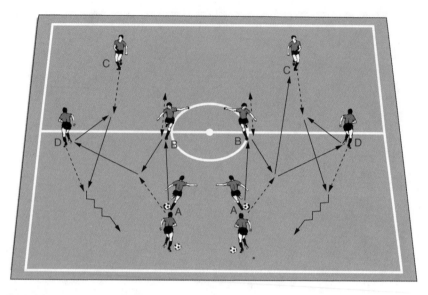

ORGANIZATION:
* Player B feints to make a run, then turns to receive the ball
* Player A passes to player B
* Player B passes back to player A, who plays a long, low pass to player D
* Player D passes to the oncoming player C
* Player C passes into space for player D to run onto
* Player D runs onto the ball and runs with it at speed, joining the group of players with the balls

INSTRUCTIONS:
* Keep your ankle stretched when passing the ball
* Keep your upper body vertical and use your arms for balance

OBJECTIVE:
* To improve passing and kicking technique

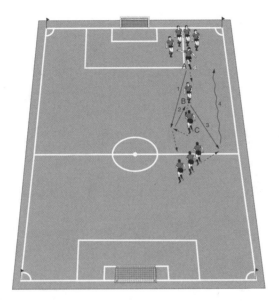

ORGANIZATION:
* 5 players stand at the starting point
* Players B and C stand behind each other in the middle, and 3 players stand near the center line
* Player A passes firmly to player C, who moves to the side
* Player C passes to player B
* Player B plays the ball diagonally to player D, who is moving to the side
* Player D runs onto the ball and sprints with it to join the group at the starting position
* Player A pushes up to take the place of player B, player B takes the place of player C, and player C takes the place of player D

INSTRUCTIONS:
* Concentrate on passing
* Pass to the receiving player's stronger foot, or pass the ball directly into the path of the receiving player
* Face the ball
* Feint to make a run before receiving the ball
* Keep moving

PASSING

OBJECTIVE:
* To improve passing and kicking technique

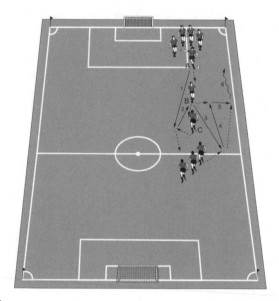

ORGANIZATION:
* 5 players stand at the starting point
* Players B and C stand behind each other in the middle and 3 players stand near the center line
* Player A passes firmly to player C, who moves to the side
* Player C passes to player B
* Player B plays the ball diagonally to player D, who is moving to the side
* Player D plays a 1-2 combination with player B and sprints with the ball to join the group at the starting position
* Player A pushes up to take the place of player B, player B takes the place of player C, and player C takes the place of player D

INSTRUCTIONS:
* Concentrate on passing
* Pass to the receiving player's stronger foot, or pass the ball directly into the path of the receiving player
* Face the ball
* Feint to make a run before receiving the ball
* Keep moving

PASSING

OBJECTIVE:
* To improve passing and kicking technique

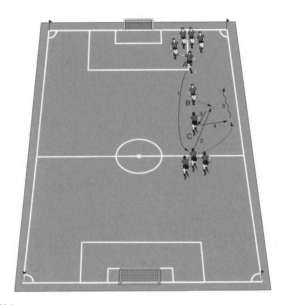

ORGANIZATION:
* 5 players stand at the starting point
* Players B and C stand behind each other in the middle and 3 players stand near the center line
* Player A plays a long pass to player D
* Player D plays the ball to player B, who passes to player C, who plays the ball to player D
* Player D joins the group of players at the starting point

VARIATION:
* Players B and C both run to the side and player D decides whether to play a 1-2 combination with player B or player C

INSTRUCTIONS:
* Concentrate on passing
* Pass to the receiving player's stronger foot, or pass the ball directly into the path of the receiving player
* Face the ball
* Feint to make a run before receiving the ball
* Keep moving

OBJECTIVE:
* To improve passing and kicking technique

ORGANIZATION:
* Player A plays the ball to player B
* Player B passes back to the incoming player A
* Player A plays the ball to player C
* Player C passes to player B
* Player B passes to player C, who runs behind the cone to receive the ball
* Player C plays the ball to player D
* Player D plays the ball to player E
* Player E passes back to the incoming player D, who shoots at the goal
* Player E fetches the ball and joins player A
* Player D takes the position of player E as the striker

VARIATION:
* Player D passes to player C
* Player C plays the ball to player E
* Player E plays the ball to player D, who shoots at the goal
or
* Player D plays a first-time pass to player E
* Player E plays the ball to winger F
* Winger F crosses the ball

OBJECTIVE:
* To improve passing and kicking technique

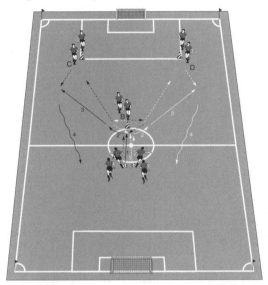

ORGANIZATION:
* 4 players stand at the starting point, 2 players at the first cone
* 2 players at each cone at the corners of the penalty area
* Work in 2 directions, i.e. with 20 players
* Carry out the sequence alternately over the right and left sides
* Player A plays the ball to player B, who controls the ball and runs with it
* Player C or player D calls for the ball
* Player B plays a firm pass over the ground to the stronger foot of player C or player D
* Player C or player D controls the ball and dribbles with it to the position of player A
* Player A is now in the position of player B, who has taken over the position of player C or player D

INSTRUCTIONS:
* Concentrate on passing
* Pass to the receiving player's stronger foot, or pass the ball directly into the path of the receiving player
* Face the ball
* Feint to make a run before receiving the ball
* Keep moving

OBJECTIVE:
* To improve passing and kicking technique

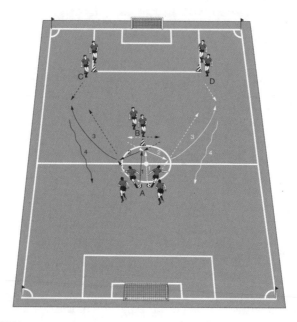

ORGANIZATION:
* 4 players stand at the starting point, 2 players at the first cone
* 2 players at each cone at the corners of the penalty area
* Work in 2 directions, i.e. with 20 players
* Carry out the sequence alternately over the right and left sides
* Player A plays the ball to player B
* Player B passes back to player A
* Player A passes through the air at random to player C or player D
* Depending on the conditional targets, player C or player D runs or sprints with the ball to the position of player A

INSTRUCTIONS:
* Concentrate on passing
* Pass to the receiving player's stronger foot, or pass the ball directly into the path of the receiving player
* Face the ball
* Feint to make a run before receiving the ball
* Keep moving

OBJECTIVE:
* To improve passing and kicking technique

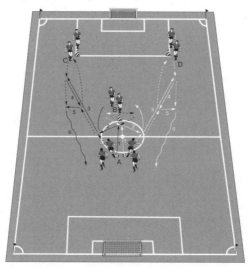

ORGANIZATION:
* 4 players stand at the starting point, 2 players at the first cone
* 2 players at each cone at the corners of the penalty area
* Work in 2 directions, i.e. with 20 players
* Carry out the sequence alternately over the right and left sides
* Player A plays the ball to player B
* Player B passes to player A
* Player A plays the ball firmly to player C or player D
* Player B calls for the ball at the right moment (not before player C or player D has controlled the ball) to play a 1-2 combination with player C or player D.
* Player A takes the position of player B, player B takes the position of player C or player D, and player C or player D dribbles the ball to the position of player A

INSTRUCTIONS:
* Concentrate on passing
* Pass to the receiving player's stronger foot, or pass the ball directly into the path of the receiving player
* Face the ball
* Feint to make a run before receiving the ball
* Keep moving

PASSING

OBJECTIVE:
* To improve passing and kicking technique

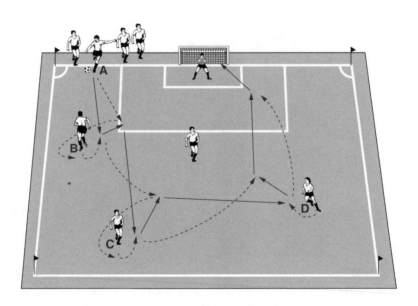

ORGANIZATION:
* Player A plays the ball to player B, who feints to make a run before receiving the ball
* Player B passes back to player A, who has made a diagonal run
* Player A plays the ball to player C, who feints to make a run before receiving the ball
* Player C plays the ball to player B, who has made a diagonal run in order to link up
* Player B passes into to the incoming player D
* Player D plays the ball into the path of player C
* Player C pushes the ball forward for player D to run onto and shoot

INSTRUCTIONS:
* At least 8 players plus a goalkeeper
* Strikers at the edge of the penalty area
* As a variation, cross the ball to one of the strikers instead of shooting

OBJECTIVE:
* To improve passing and kicking technique

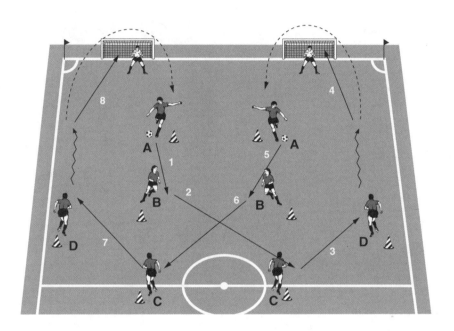

ORGANIZATION:
* Player A plays the ball to player B
* Player B plays the ball diagonally to player C
* Player C passes to player D
* Player D dribbles toward the goal and shoots.
* Carry out this drill on both the right and left sides

INSTRUCTIONS:
* Concentrate on passing
* Pass to the receiving player's stronger foot, or pass the ball directly into the path of the receiving player
* Face the ball
* Feint to make a run before receiving the ball
* Keep moving

OBJECTIVE:
* To improve passing and kicking technique

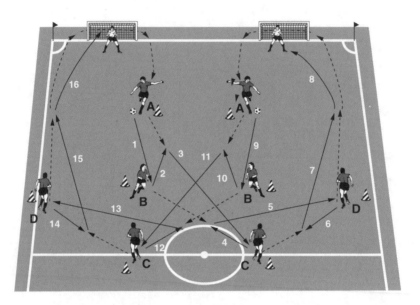

ORGANIZATION:
* Player A plays the ball to player B
* Player B plays the ball back to the incoming player A
* Player A passes to player C
* Player C plays the ball to the incoming player B
* Player B passes to player D
* Player D plays the ball to the incoming player C
* Player D shoots at goal
* Carry out this drill on both the right and left sides

INSTRUCTIONS:
* Concentrate on passing
* Pass to the receiving player's stronger foot, or pass the ball directly into the path of the receiving player
* Face the ball
* Feint to make a run before receiving the ball
* Keep moving

PASSING

47

OBJECTIVE:
* To improve passing and kicking technique

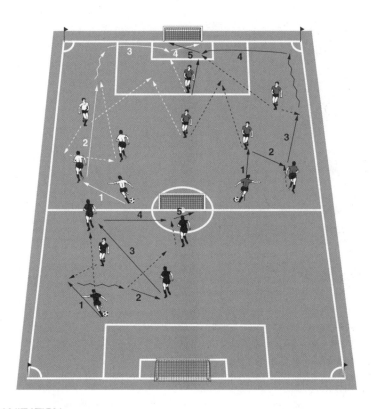

ORGANIZATION:
* Field with 3 goals
* Start the drill alternately over the right and left flanks
* Each player starts from his or her own position

INSTRUCTIONS:
* Put the emphasis on the attacking run down the flank
* Put the emphasis on the midfielder who gets forward in front of goal
* Put the emphasis on the advancing fullback
* Coach the players in specific tasks relating to specific situations

PASSING

OBJECTIVE:

• To improve passing and shooting when under pressure from an opponent

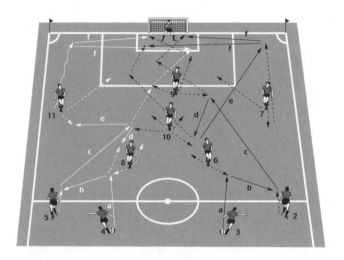

ORGANIZATION:

• The central defender plays the ball forward to the midfielder (the midfielder makes a run to escape his marker)
• The midfielder plays the ball back to the defender
• The defender plays the ball to the attacking midfielder (the midfielder makes a run to escape his marker)
• The attacking midfielder plays the ball to the supporting midfielder (who is unmarked)
• The supporting midfielder passes to the winger, and dribbles forward and crosses the ball without being challenged
• Player 9 always takes up position at the near post and player 10 at the far post

INSTRUCTIONS:

• Shout loudly and clearly for the ball (for example, back/to feet/long/ take your man)
• Cross the ball firmly

VARIATION:

• Play the ball to the striker (9), who must feint to make a run to escape his marker. The hanging striker (10) gives support. Pass into space on the wing.

PASSING

OBJECTIVE:
* To improve passing and kicking technique

ORGANIZATION:
* Half field
* 10 players versus 4 defenders
* Players move up 1 position after each sequence
* Left and right alternately
* Player A passes to player B
* Player B plays the ball back to player A
* Player A passes to player C
* Player C passes to player B
* Player B passes to player D and player C runs down the wing to support player D
* Players C and D exploit their 2v1 advantage to take the ball past the defender
* Player C passes to player E
* Player E shoots at goal
* The offside rule applies when players C and D try to exploit their 2v1 advantage
* The defending fullbacks stand on the end line and may only run toward the attackers when player B passes to player D

PASSING

OBJECTIVE:
* To improve passing to a striker
* To improve the timing of passes to a striker
* To improve passing into the path of another player
* To improve the ability to hit a pass to a striker with just the right speed

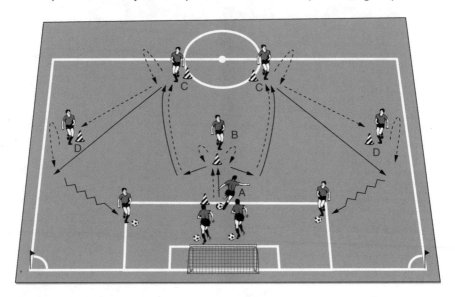

ORGANIZATION:
* Half field
* Players stand at the cones
* Player B feints to make a run
* Player A passes to player B
* Player B plays the ball back to the incoming player A
* Player C feints to make a run
* Player A passes to player C
* Player D feints to make a run
* Player C passes to player D
* Player D dribbles forward and joins the group at cone A
* Carry out over the right and left sides
* Players move up 1 position after each sequence

INSTRUCTIONS:
* Coach the players continuously on how they carry out their tasks
* Players must learn to understand each other's intentions
* Emphasis on specific tasks in specific situations

PASSING

OBJECTIVE:
* To improve passing to a striker
* To improve the timing of passes to a striker
* To improve passing into the path of another player
* To improve the ability to hit a pass to a striker with just the right speed

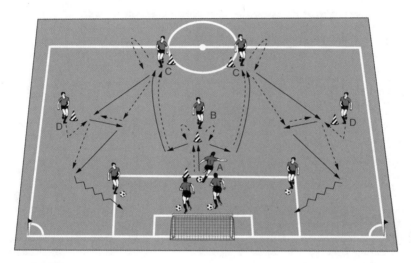

ORGANIZATION:
* Half field
* Players stand at the cones
* Player B feints to make a run
* Player A passes to player B
* Player B plays the ball back to the incoming player A
* Player C feints to make a run
* Player A passes to player C
* Player D makes a forward run and calls for the ball to be into his path
* Player C passes into the path of player D
* Player D plays a 1-2 combination with player C
* Carry out over the right and left sides
* Players move up one position after each sequence

INSTRUCTIONS:
* When the pass is played to the striker, call "turn"
* The striker does not pass the ball back to the passer but turns and passes to the following player
* As the end of the drill approaches, allow the players to make their own choices

OBJECTIVE:
* To improve passing to a striker
* To improve the timing of passes to a striker
* To improve passing into the path of another player
* To improve the ability to hit a pass to a striker with just the right speed

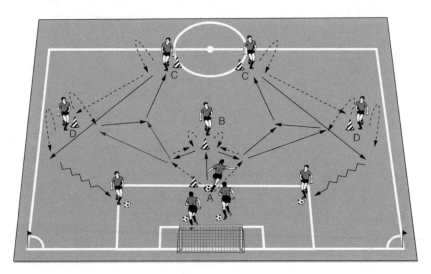

ORGANIZATION:
* Half field
* Players stand at the cones
* Player B feints to make a run
* Player A passes to player B
* Player B plays the ball back to the incoming player A
* Player A plays a 1-2 combination with player D
* Player A passes to player C
* Player C passes to player D, who is making a forward run
* Player D dribbles forward and joins the group at cone A
* Carry out over the right and left sides
* Players move up one position after each sequence

INSTRUCTIONS:
* When the pass is played to the striker, call "turn"
* The striker does not pass the ball back to the passer but turns and passes to the following player
* As the end of the drill approaches, allow the players to make their own choices

PASSING

OBJECTIVE:
- To improve passing and kicking technique and shooting at goal

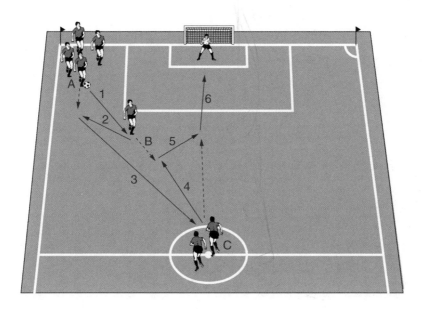

ORGANIZATION:
- Player A feints to make a run but then passes to player B
- Player B plays the ball back to player A
- Player A passes to player C
- Player C plays the ball to player B, who has run into space to receive the pass
- Player B plays the ball into the path of the incoming player C, who takes it forward and shoots at goal

INSTRUCTIONS:
- Carry out over the right and left sides
- Players move up one position after each sequence

OBJECTIVE:
* To improve passing and kicking technique and shooting at goal

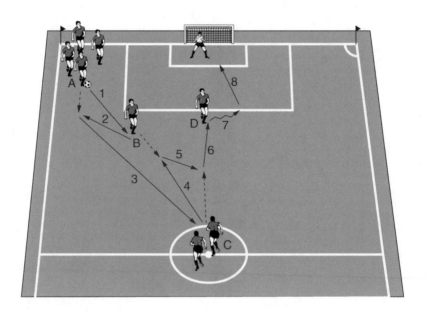

ORGANIZATION:
* Player A feints to make a run but then passes to player B
* Player B plays the ball back to player A
* Player A passes to player C
* Player C plays the ball back to player B, who has run into space to receive the pass
* Player B plays the ball into the path of the incoming player C
* Player C passes to player D, who takes the ball forward and shoots at goal

INSTRUCTIONS:
* Carry out over the right and left sides
* Players move up one position after each sequence

PASSING

55

OBJECTIVE:
* To improve passing and kicking technique and shooting at goal

ORGANIZATION:
* Player A feints to make a run but then passes to player B
* Player B plays the ball back to player A
* Player C moves so that he is not blocking the line between player A and player D.
* Player A passes to player D
* Player D plays a 1-2 combination with player C
* Player D plays a 1-2 combination with player B
* Player D plays the ball to player E, who takes it forward and shoots at goal

INSTRUCTIONS:
* Carry out over the right and left sides
* Players move up one position after each sequence

Chapter Three

SHOOTING
56-66

OBJECTIVE:
 • To improve shooting at goal after a dribble

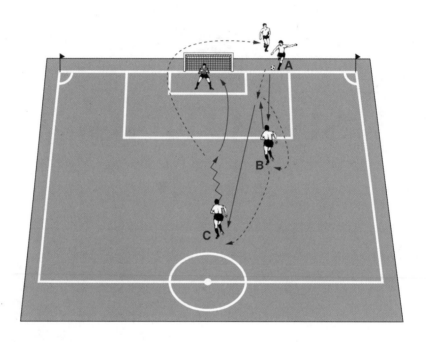

ORGANIZATION:
 • Player A passes to player B
 • Player B plays the ball back to player A
 • Player A passes to player C
 • Player C dribbles forward with the ball and shoots at goal
 • Players move up one position after each sequence

INSTRUCTIONS:
 • Call for the ball
 • Look to see where the goalkeeper is positioned

OBJECTIVE:
* To improve shooting at goal after a pass

ORGANIZATION:
* Player A passes to player B
* Player B plays the ball back to player A
* Player A passes to player C
* Player C passes to player B
* Player B plays the ball square for player C
* Player C shoots at goal
* Players move up one position after each sequence

INSTRUCTIONS:
* Call for the ball
* Look to see where the goalkeeper is positioned

OBJECTIVE:
* To improve shooting at goal after a dribble

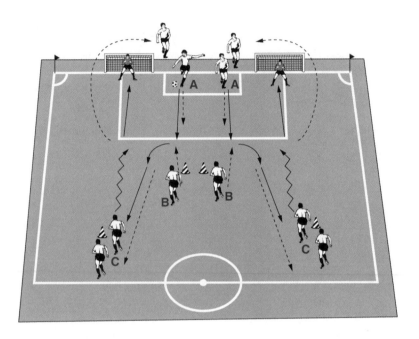

ORGANIZATION:
* Player A passes to player B
* Player B half-turns as he takes the ball
* Player B passes to player C
* Player C dribbles toward the goal and shoots
* Players move up one position after each sequence

INSTRUCTIONS:
* Call for the ball
* Look to see where the goalkeeper is positioned

OBJECTIVE:
* To improve defensive skills

ORGANIZATION:
* Player A passes to the incoming player B
* Player B plays the ball back to the incoming player A
* Player A shoots at goal
* Players move up one position after each sequence

INSTRUCTIONS:
* Choose a position between the ball and the goal
* You must be moving forward when you receive the ball
* Don't control the ball; try to play one-touch or at most two-touch soccer
* Look around you - don't just look at the ball
* Accelerate when you dribble - be more aggressive

VARIATIONS:
Variation 1
* Player A runs along a different line; player B must look to see where player A is
Variation 2
* Player A becomes a defender after he has passed to player B

SHOOTING

OBJECTIVE:
* To improve shooting at goal after a 1-2 combination

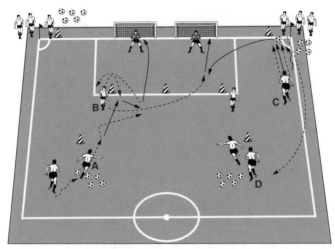

ORGANIZATION:
* Field with 2 goals (4 yards apart)
* At least 12 players and 2 goalkeepers
* Player A plays the ball to player B from a stationary position or after a dribble. Player B feints to make a run before receiving the ball.
* Player A feints to run in 1 direction then runs into space to take a return pass from player B
* Player A shoots with right-footed (inside of foot, or instep)
* Player A runs to the position of player B
* Player B runs behind player A, then runs forward and calls for a low, medium-high or high cross from player C
* Player C crosses (stationary ball, or after a run or a dribble)
* Player B shoots and joins the group behind player C
* Player C goes to the position of player D
* Repeat the sequence starting from this position

INSTRUCTIONS:
* Goalkeepers swap goals regularly
* Pass after a dribble
* 1-touch pass/receiving and running with the ball/ through pass
* Shoot with inside of foot or instep; volley or head the ball
* Feint to make a run (keep your eye on the ball), both before receiving the ball and before shooting after receiving a return pass

SHOOTING

OBJECTIVE:
* To improve shooting on the turn/controlling and moving with the ball

ORGANIZATION:
* Field with 2 goals (4 yards apart)
* At least 12 players and 2 goalkeepers
* Player A plays the ball to player B from a stationary position or after a dribble. Player B feints to make a run before receiving the ball.
* Player B makes a half turn to his left as he receives the ball, takes a few steps and shoots at goal

INSTRUCTIONS:
* Goalkeepers swap goals regularly
* Pass after a dribble
* 1-touch pass/ controlling and moving with the ball/through pass
* Look around - don't just look at the ball
* Shoot with inside of foot or instep; volley or head the ball
* Feint to make a run (keep your eye on the ball), both before receiving the ball and before shooting after receiving a return pass
* Make a good run before receiving the cross
* Time the cross properly
* React to a rebound
* Circulate the ball quickly
* Before shooting, look to see where the goalkeeper is positioned
* Run through to the next position after the sequence is complete

SHOOTING

OBJECTIVE:
* To improve shooting on the turn/controlling and moving with the ball

ORGANIZATION:
* Field with 2 goals
* At least 12 players and 2 goalkeepers
* Player A plays the ball to player B from a stationary position or after a dribble. Player B feints to make a run before receiving the ball.
* Player A makes a half turn to his right as he receives the ball (inside or outside of foot) and plays the ball square for player A to shoot at goal

INSTRUCTIONS:
* Goalkeepers swap goals regularly
* Pass after a dribble
* 1-touch pass/ controlling and moving with the ball/through pass
* Shoot with inside of foot or instep; volley or head the ball
* Feint to make a run (keep your eye on the ball), both before receiving the ball and before shooting after receiving a return pass
* Make a good run before receiving the cross
* Time the cross properly
* React to a rebound
* Circulate the ball quickly
* Before shooting, look to see where the goalkeeper is positioned
* Run through to the next position after the sequence is complete

OBJECTIVE:
* To improve finishing from a low cross (shot), medium-high cross (volley) or high cross (header)

ORGANIZATION:
* Field with 2 goals
* At least 12 players and 2 goalkeepers
* Player A plays the ball to player B from a stationary position or after a dribble. Player B feints to make a run before receiving the ball.
* Player B plays the ball back to player A, who plays the ball forward for B to shoot, side-foot or chip the ball at goal

INSTRUCTIONS:
* Goalkeepers swap goals regularly
* Pass after a dribble
* 1-touch pass/ controlling and moving with the ball/through pass
* Shoot with inside of foot or instep; volley or head the ball
* Feint to make a run (keep your eye on the ball), both before receiving the ball and before shooting after receiving a return pass
* Make a good run before receiving the cross
* Time the cross properly
* React to a rebound
* Circulate the ball quickly
* Before shooting, look to see where the goalkeeper is positioned
* Run through to the next position after the sequence is complete

OBJECTIVE:
* To improve shooting after receiving a pass

ORGANIZATION:
* Player 7 passes to player 11
* If player 11 runs toward player 7 first, he wants the ball played forward to run onto. If he makes a forward run first, he wants the ball played to his feet
* Player 11 always receives the ball when he is in motion, never stationary
* Player 11 crosses to player 9 at the near post or player 10 near the penalty spot or player 8 at the far post
* Never stand in line in front of the goal
* Practice the move over the right and the left flank
* Alternate between running onto the ball and making the forward run before receiving the ball

INSTRUCTIONS:
* Call for the ball
* Look to see where the goalkeeper is positioned

SHOOTING

OBJECTIVE:
* To improve shooting after receiving a pass

ORGANIZATION:
* Each striker starts with 3 balls
* In sequence, the goalkeeper plays the ball high or low, or bounces it to each striker
* The striker must control the ball with his first touch so that he can shoot at goal with his second touch
* Always receive the ball facing the goal
* Always keep the ball within reach
* Use both the right and left foot to control the ball and shoot
* Make the drill competitive when possible

INSTRUCTIONS:
* Call for the ball
* Look to see where the goalkeeper is positioned

SHOOTING

OBJECTIVE:
* To improve shooting at goal

ORGANIZATION:
* Midfielder 7 or 6 passes to striker 9, who feints to make a run before receiving the ball
* As the pass is made, the winger 11 or 8 makes a diagonal run forward
* Striker 9 lays the ball off into the path of the winger and turns to run at goal, so that he shields the ball from an imaginary opponent who might want to prevent the winger from shooting at goal
* The winger shoots
* Player 9 must be ready to score from a rebound

INSTRUCTIONS:
* Call for the ball
* Look to see where the goalkeeper is positioned

Chapter Four

COMBINATION PLAYS

67-77

OBJECTIVE:
• To exploit a 2 against 1 situation under pressure from behind

ORGANIZATION:
• Player A passes to striker B
• Player B passes to the oncoming player C
• Player C plays the ball square for the oncoming player B
• Player C and player B try to exploit the 2v1 situation to attack the goal
• Player A runs as fast as possible round the cone and helps the defender
• Play alternately over the right and left sides of the area

INSTRUCTIONS:
• Striker C must run into space to escape his marker at the right moment
• Pass directly to striker C's stronger foot
• Striker C either plays a return pass or goes for goal on his own, depending on what the defender does.

OBJECTIVE:
* To improve attacking build-up out of defense down the center of the field

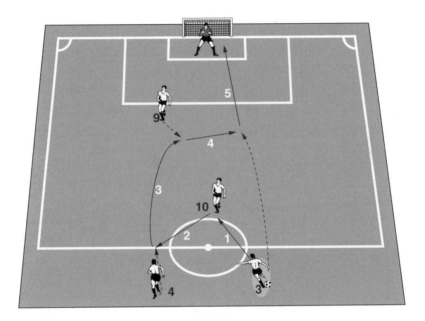

ORGANIZATION:
* The build-up of each attack starts with the central defenders, with each player taking up his own position: 2 central defenders (3 and 4), the central midfielder (10) and 1 striker (9)
* Player 3 passes to player 10
* Player 3 runs toward player 9
* Player 10 passes to player 4, who plays a long ball forward to player 9
* Player 9 plays the ball into the path of the oncoming player 3, who shoots from 20 yards

OBJECTIVE:

• To improve attacking build-up out of defense down the center of the field

ORGANIZATION:

• The build-up of each attack starts with the central defenders, with each player taking up his own position: 2 central defenders (3 and 4), the central midfielder (10) and 1 striker (9)
• Player 3 passes to player 10 and runs forward
• Player 10 plays the ball back to player 3 and makes a diagonal forward run to the right
• Player 3 plays a long ball forward to player 9
• Player 4 asks for and receives a square pass from player 9
• Player 4 can go through and shoot, or he can play the ball square to player 10

OBJECTIVE:

◆ To improve attacking build-up out of defense down the center of the field

ORGANIZATION:

◆ The build-up of each attack starts with the central defenders, with each player taking up his own position: 2 central defenders (3 and 4), the central midfielder (10), 1 striker (9) and a central defender (5) of the defending team
◆ The goalkeeper passes to player 5, receives a return pass and kicks the ball forward
◆ Player 5 goes to mark player 9
◆ The attacking team gains possession
◆ Player 3 passes to player 10
◆ Player 10 plays the ball back to player 3 and makes a diagonal sprint to the right
◆ Player 3 plays a long ball forward to player 9, who, together with player 10, tries to quickly exploit the 2v1 situation

COMBINATION PLAYS

OBJECTIVE:
* To create a scoring chance from a build-up

ORGANIZATION:
* Player A passes to player B
* Player B controls the ball with the inside of his right foot and makes a half turn to his right
* Player B passes to player C
* Player C passes with the inside of his left foot to the supporting player A
* Player A passes to player D
* Player D passes plays the ball with the inside of his right foot to player B
* Defender E challenges player D during this action
* Player B plays the ball into the corner of the field where the incoming player D crosses to player F
* Players A, B, D and E return to their starting positions
* Player C replaces player F
* Now player D makes a run down the wing instead of passing to player B

OBJECTIVE:
* To create a scoring chance from a build-up

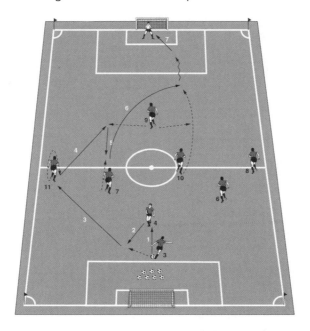

ORGANIZATION:
* Player 3 passes to player 4
* Player 4 passes square to the incoming player 3
* Player 3 passes to player 11
* Player 11 plays a diagonal pass to player 9, who comes to meet the ball
* Player 9 passes to player 7
* Player 7 passes to player 10, who has made a forward run behind the back of player 9
* Player 10 shoots at goal

INSTRUCTIONS:
* Practice this drill on the right and left flanks
* Forward run by the third man
* Play the ball to the receiver's strongest foot
* The wingers 11 and 8 feint to make a run before receiving the ball
* Timing of the run by striker 9
* Timing of the runs by midfielders 7 and 6
* Run by midfielder 10

OBJECTIVE:
* To create a scoring chance from a build-up

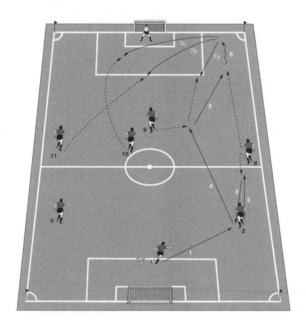

ORGANIZATION:
* The goalkeeper plays the ball to fullback 2
* Player 8 feints to make a run, then receives the ball from player 2
* Player 8 plays the ball back to player 2
* Player 2 passes to striker 9, who runs to meet the ball
* Player 9 passes into the path of player 8, who has made a run down the wing
* Player 8 dribbles the ball to the end line and crosses to player 9, player 10 or player 11

INSTRUCTIONS:
* Attacking build-up over the players on the wings (5 and 2)
* Positioning of players 10, 11 and 9 in front of the goal
* Concentrate on passing
* Wingers 11 and 8 feint to make a run before receiving the ball
* Timing of the run by striker 9
* Timing of the run by midfielders 10
* Positions of the players in front of the goal

OBJECTIVE:
* To create a scoring chance from a build-up

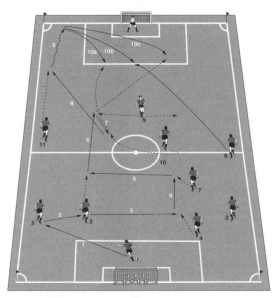

ORGANIZATION:
* The goalkeeper plays the ball to player 5
* Player 5 passes to player 3
* Player 3 plays the ball square to player 4
* Player 4 passes to player 7
* Player 7 passes to the oncoming player 3
* Player 3 passes to striker 9
* Player 9 lays the ball back to player 10, who feints to make a run before receiving the ball and then passes forward to winger 11
* Player 11 takes the ball to the end line and then passes to player 10, player 9 or player 8

INSTRUCTIONS:
* Involve additional player 3 or 4 in the build-up in the midfield
* Wing play
* Concentrate on passing
* Player 10 feints to make a run before receiving the ball
* Runs by wingers 11 and 8
* Timing of the run by striker 9
* Positions of the players in front of the goal

COMBINATION PLAYS

OBJECTIVE:
* To score as quickly as possible from fixed positions

ORGANIZATION:
Half field

INSTRUCTIONS:
* The goalkeeper starts the attack by kicking the ball out to player 2, 4 or 3
* From free play to 2-touch play and 1-touch play
* Add 1 or 2 defenders in the penalty area
* Assign specific tasks, e.g. team can attack after pass from player 5, only players 7 and 10 are allowed to score, a midfielder must be included in the combination play, a goal must be scored within 10 seconds, etc.

OBJECTIVE:
* The attackers try to take the ball past the defenders as quickly as possible and score a goal
* The defenders try to win the ball

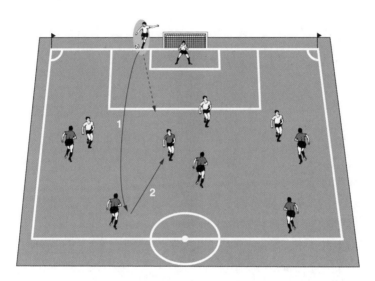

ORGANIZATION:
* Defending team: goalkeeper and 4 defenders
* Attacking team: 3 attackers, 1 attacking midfielder and 2 defensive midfielders
* The central defender (right) plays the ball from the end line to the defensive left-midfielder of the attacking team
* There is now a 6v4 situation
* The defensive midfielder can pass to one of the other midfielders or to one of the 3 attackers

INSTRUCTIONS:
* The 2 defensive midfielders can only play the ball forward
* When a defensive midfielder has the ball, the defenders take up their positions and pressure the player with the ball
* The task of the attackers is to run into space
* The attacking midfielder can link up with them
* Naturally it is the objective of the attacking team to take the ball past the defenders and score a goal, and it is the task of the defending team to restrict the attacking team's passing options and win the ball

OBJECTIVE:
* The attackers try to take the ball past the defenders as quickly as possible and score a goal
* The defenders try to win the ball

ORGANIZATION:
* Defending team: goalkeeper, 4 defenders and 2 defensive midfielders
* Attacking team: 3 attackers, 1 attacking midfielder and 2 defensive midfielders
* The central defender (right) plays the ball from the end line to the defensive left-midfielder of the attacking team
* There is now a 6v4 situation
* The defensive midfielder can pass to one of the other midfielders or to one of the 3 attackers

INSTRUCTIONS:
* The 2 defensive midfielders can only play the ball forward
* When a defensive midfielder has the ball, the defenders take up their positions and pressure the player with the ball
* The task of the attackers is to run into space
* The attacking midfielder can link up with them

Chapter Five

SMALL SIDED
GAMES
78-180

OBJECTIVE:

◆ To take the ball past an opponent

ORGANIZATION:

◆ Field measuring 30 x 40 yards
◆ 2 teams of 3 field players and 1 goalkeeper
◆ 1v1 until the ball goes over a line
◆ Call clearly which team starts
◆ Keep score

INSTRUCTIONS::

◆ Head directly for goal (and your opponent)
◆ Do not turn your back on your opponent - this causes you to lose speed
◆ Try to score with your weaker foot occasionally

OBJECTIVE:
* To take the ball past an opponent in a 1v1 situation

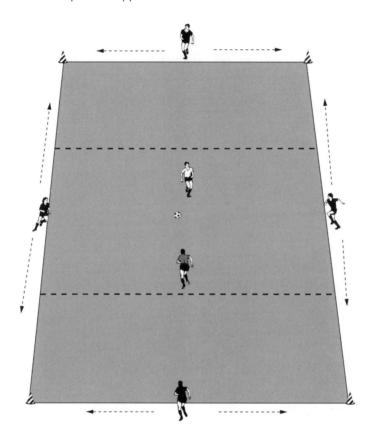

ORGANIZATION:
* The lay-off players can touch the ball twice each time they receive it
* Play at speed; seek the correct forward player
* Lay-off players can play together

INSTRUCTIONS:
* Play the ball to the lay-off player in the most distant zone
* If he can play the ball back with his first touch, he scores 1 point
* Pass over the ground or through the air

OBJECTIVE:
* To improve 1v1 play

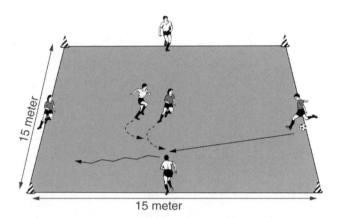

ORGANIZATION:
* 2 groups of 3 players
* One player stands in the middle and tries to win the 1v1 duel
* If he loses he becomes a defender
* After 2 minutes, switch with the lay-off players

INSTRUCTIONS:
* Watch how your opponent dribbles; if he dribbles fast, react when he is further away
* Move on the balls of the feet with a slightly crouching posture, so that you can move quickly in any direction
* Cover the direct route to goal
* Take up position relative to the attacker so that you can intercept the pass to the attacker
* Try to pressure your opponent so that he does not have the time or the space to make a run
* Try to force your opponent toward the side line

OBJECTIVE:
* To improve 1v1 play

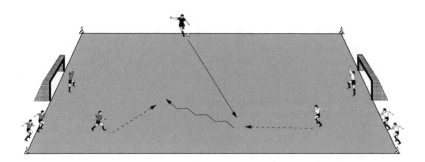

ORGANIZATION:
* 2 players call for the ball
* The coach passes the ball from the side line
* 1v1. The objective is to score in the opponent's full size goal, which is defended by a goalkeeper.

INSTRUCTIONS:
* Watch how your opponent dribbles; if he dribbles fast, react when he is further away
* Move on the balls of the feet with a slightly crouching posture, so that you can move quickly in any direction
* Cover the direct route to goal
* Take up position relative to the attacker so that you can intercept the pass to the attacker
* Try to pressure your opponent so that he does not have the time or the space to make a run
* Try to force your opponent toward the side line

OBJECTIVE:
* Conditioning for strength in the duel
* To practice shielding the ball

ORGANIZATION:
* Half field
* 2 groups

INSTRUCTIONS:
* The coach plays the ball forward
* The players sprint round the cone
* 1v1
* The winner of the 1v1 duel scores

OBJECTIVE:
- To improve 1v1 play

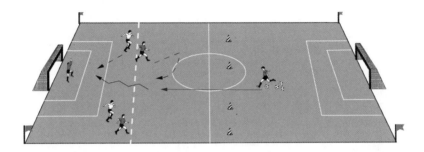

ORGANIZATION:
- 2 players stand about 20 yards from the goal
- The attacker tries to take the ball and score
- If the defender intercepts the ball, he tries to score in one of the small goals

INSTRUCTIONS:
- Watch how your opponent dribbles; if he dribbles fast, react when he is further away
- Move on the balls of the feet with a slightly crouching posture, so that you can move quickly in any direction
- Cover the direct route to goal
- Take up position relative to the attacker so that you can intercept the pass to the attacker
- Try to pressure your opponent so that he does not have the time or the space to make a run
- Try to force your opponent toward the side line

OBJECTIVE:
* To improve 1v1 play

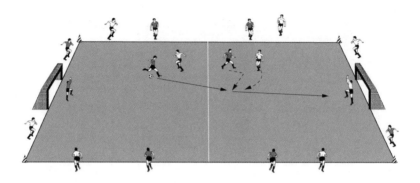

ORGANIZATION:
* 2 opponents play against each other in each half
* The players may not leave their half of the field
* The defender passes to the attacker, who tries to score

INSTRUCTIONS:
* Watch how your opponent dribbles; if he dribbles fast, react when he is further away
* Move on the balls of the feet with a slightly crouching posture, so that you can move quickly in any direction
* Cover the direct route to goal
* Take up position relative to the attacker so that you can intercept the pass to the attacker
* Try to pressure your opponent so that he does not have the time or the space to make a run
* Try to force your opponent toward the side line

OBJECTIVE:
* To improve 1v1 play

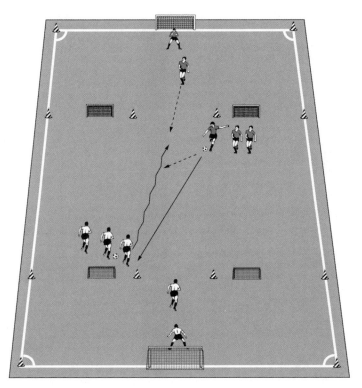

ORGANIZATION:
* 16 players, 2 are goalkeepers
* 2 teams of 7 players
* 1 full-size portable goal and 14 cones

INSTRUCTIONS:
1v1 duel with the opponent facing you
* 1 team plays the ball to the opposing team and a 1v1 duel then ensues
* The player who wins the duel in the rectangle (when he passes the imaginary line of the rectangle) takes on the defender
* The attacker scores in the full-size goal and the defender in one of the 2 small goals
* The other team then plays the ball in to its opponents

SMALL SIDED GAMES (1V1)

OBJECTIVE:
- To improve 1v1 play

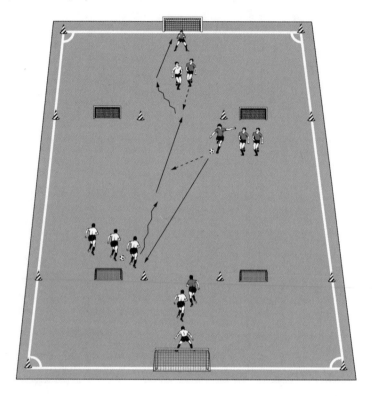

ORGANIZATION:
- 16 players, 2 are goalkeepers
- 2 teams of 7 players
- 1 full-size portable goal and 14 cones

INSTRUCTIONS:
1v1 duel with the opponent facing you
- At a sign from the coach, 2 players sprint round a cone
- The ball is played in alternately by the 2 teams
- The team that plays the ball in scores in the full-size goal and the other team scores in one of the 2 small goals

OBJECTIVE:
* To improve 1v1 play

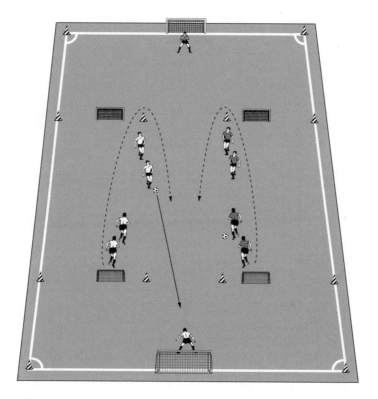

ORGANIZATION:
* 16 players, 2 are goalkeepers
* 2 teams of 7 players
* 1 full-size portable goal and 14 cones

INSTRUCTIONS:
1v1 duel in defense
* At a sign from the coach, 2 players sprint round a cone
* The ball is played in alternately by the 2 teams
* After the 1v1 duel, the winner of the duel plays the ball in to his teammate and another 1v1 duel ensues
* The attacker scores in the full-size goal
* The defender scores in one of the 2 small goals

OBJECTIVE:
* To improve 1v1 play

ORGANIZATION:
* 4 or 5 small goals and 1 full-size goal
* 8 to 10 players, or even 12, and 1 goalkeeper
* An attacker starts with the ball at his foot, facing a defender
* The attacker scores in the full-size goal
* The defender scores in one of the small goals
* After each goalscoring attempt (maximum of 10 seconds), the players move up one position
* Each player keeps his score
* After one series the defenders move one position to the right

INSTRUCTIONS:
* Attackers: Do not stand still with the ball
* Defenders: Watch the ball

OBJECTIVE:
* To learn how to take advantage of a 2v2 situation

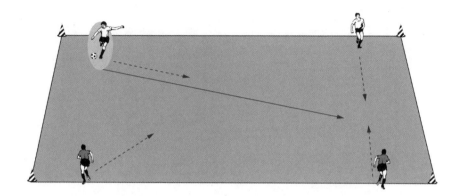

ORGANIZATION:
* Start by playing the ball diagonally
* The other player pressures the player with the ball

Attacking
* Run to meet the ball when the first pass is made
* The player with the ball seeks a 1v1 duel with his opponent
* The player with the ball moves inside and his teammate moves up on the outside
* 1-2 combination

Defending
* The player who plays the ball in covers the other defender's back
* If the attackers take the ball past the other defender, the covering player must be able to win the ball or hold up the attacker

SMALL SIDED GAMES (2V2)

OBJECTIVE:
* To improve positional play

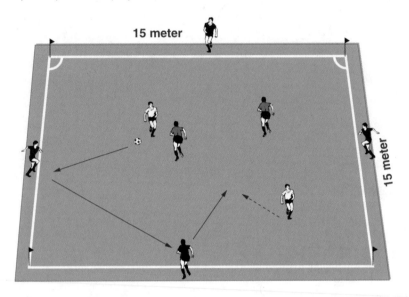

15 meter

15 meter

ORGANIZATION:
* A field measuring 15 x 15 yards
* 2 teams of 2 players and 4 lay-off players
* The lay-off players can play the ball round a maximum of 3 times
* Choose position
* Face the ball
* Play the ball to the correct foot
* Anticipate the moment when the ball will be laid off
* Run into space from behind the opponent's back

SMALL SIDED GAMES (2V2)

OBJECTIVE:
* Attackers: To learn how to take the ball past an opponent, individually or collectively
* Defenders: To learn how to win the ball

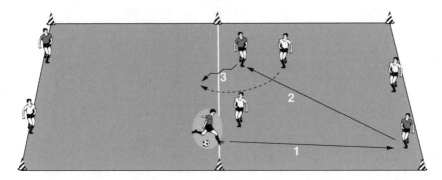

ORGANIZATION:
* A field measuring 15 x 20 yards
* 2 teams of 4 players
* 2 players from each team are on the field
* The other 2 players stand on the end line

INSTRUCTIONS:
* The team in possession must try to play the ball to the 2 players on the end line as often as possible
* Each pass to a player on the end line scores 1 point

OBJECTIVE:
To score as quickly as possible

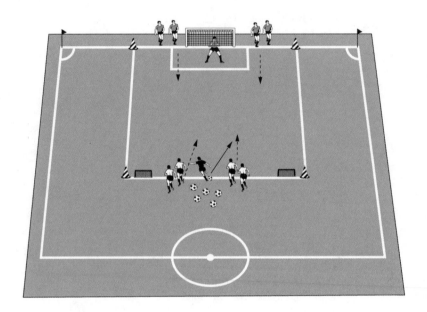

ORGANIZATION:
* A field twice the size of the penalty area
* 1 full size goal defended by a goalkeeper
* 2 small goals on the other end line
* The coach plays the balls in
* 2 attackers start from the end line
* 2 defenders start at the same time
* Score within 45 seconds

INSTRUCTIONS:
* Coach the players on how to defend properly
* The attackers and defenders switch roles when possession changes

OBJECTIVE:
To learn how to take advantage of a 2v2 situation

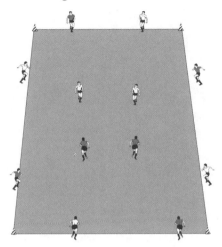

ORGANIZATION:
* A field measuring 15 x 20 yards
* 2 teams of 6 players (2v2 on the inside for 90 seconds each)
* Players assigned into pairs
* The lay-off players are allowed only 1 touch

VARIATION:
* The ball can be played twice from lay-off player to lay-off player, then back to the pair
* The ball can be played once from lay-off player to lay-off player
* The ball must be laid off to a third player (not the player the ball came from; lay-off players can play the ball to each other twice)

INSTRUCTIONS:
In possession
* Good team shape
* Shooting
* Scoring
* Transition when possession changes
Opponents in possession
* Close marking
* Preventing attackers from shooting and scoring
* Transition when possession changes

OBJECTIVE:
To learn how to take advantage of a 2v2 situation

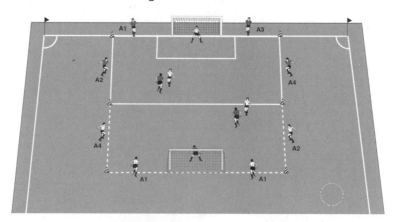

ORGANIZATION:
* A field twice the size of the penalty area
* 2 minutes of work
* Lay-off players beside the goal and on the side lines
* Lay-off players can touch the ball once only
* Lay-off player A1 can play the ball to lay-off player A2, who must then cross it
* Lay-off player A4 can then come in from the flank and score, and vice-versa
* Lay-off player A2 then comes in from the flank
* Players assigned into pairs

INSTRUCTIONS:
[First column]
In possession
* Good team shape
* Shooting
* Scoring
* Transition when possession changes
[Second column]
Opponents in possession
* Close marking
* Preventing attackers from shooting and scoring
* Transition when possession changes

OBJECTIVE:
Learning to take advantage of a 2v2 situation

ORGANIZATION:
- A field twice the size of the penalty area
- 2 minutes of work
- Lay-off players beside the goal and on the side lines
- Lay-off players can touch the ball once only
- Lay-off player A1 can play the ball to lay-off player A2, who must then cross it
- Lay-off player A4 can then come in from the flank and score, and vice-versa
- Lay-off player A2 then comes in from the flank
- Players assigned into pairs

INSTRUCTIONS:
[First column]
In possession
- Good team shape
- Shooting
- Scoring
- Transition when possession changes

[Second column]
Opponents in possession
- Close marking
- Preventing attackers from shooting and scoring
- Transition when possession changes

OBJECTIVE:
* Learning to take the ball past an opponent

ORGANIZATION:
* A field measuring 40 x 20 yards with a zone 3 yards wide at each end
* 2 teams of 3 players try to dribble the ball into their end zone
* When a player passes the ball, his teammates must be behind the ball
* The game can be restarted with a dribble

INSTRUCTIONS:
* You can only gain ground and score by dribbling
* The teammates of the player in possession must ensure that he always has the option of passing the ball to the right or left
* 1v1 situations can be created by switching the play

SMALL SIDED GAMES (3V3) 9

OBJECTIVE:

[left]
- ◆ To learn how to get into the final third
- ◆ To improve combination play

[right]
- ◆ Getting into good positions
- ◆ Switching quickly from defense to attack and vice versa when possession changes

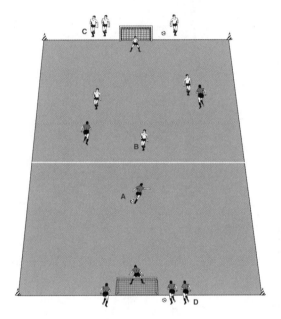

ORGANIZATION:
- ◆ The size of the field depends on the level of skill of the players
- ◆ The smaller the field, the greater the level of difficulty and the faster the players have to react

INSTRUCTIONS:
- ◆ You play 3v3 with 2 teams of 6 players
- ◆ When team A has possession, it tries to score as quickly as possible
- ◆ If team A scores, team B is replaced by team C, which is waiting behind the goal
- ◆ The teams also switch if one team shoots over or wide of the goal
- ◆ The team in possession can only play the ball forward into the final third (i.e. not back to the goalkeeper)

OBJECTIVE:
* To win the ball and switch quickly from defense to attack

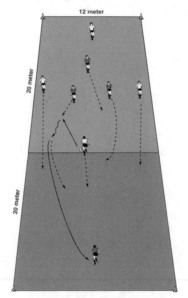

ORGANIZATION:
* A field measuring 12 x 40 yards
* 8 players
* Competitive game: Passing the ball round 10 times scores 1 point

INSTRUCTIONS:
* The attackers win the ball and play it into the other zone
* The 3 attackers and the 3 defenders join in
* The attacking team plays 4v3 in the bottom zone, where the defending team has to win the ball and play it into the other zone

Technical
* Controlling a pass
* Laying the ball off
* Using both feet
* Circulating the ball quickly
* Reacting quickly
* Linking up rapidly and creating a good team shape

Tactical
* Switching quickly from attack to defense
* Preventing a long forward pass

OBJECTIVE:
• To find space with the ball when under pressure

ORGANIZATION:
• A field measuring 15 x 12 yards
• Fixed pairs of players
• Players must have at least 2 contacts each time they receive the ball
• Defenders try to dribble over one of the end lines

INSTRUCTIONS:
• Look around to see where there is space before receiving the ball
• Move away from your opponent as you receive the ball
• Feint before receiving the ball
• Give the player in possession enough room to find space with the ball

OBJECTIVE:
* To improve technique
* To carry out specific tasks
* To learn how to play under pressure

ORGANIZATION:
* Half field
* 6 players
* 1 goalkeeper
* 1 ball (10 extra balls)
* 10 to 20 repeats
* Practice for 10 to 15 minutes
* The goalkeeper (1) kicks the ball to player 2, 3, 4 or 5, depending on the situation
* After the goalkeeper kicks the ball, he goes to the same side as the ball
* Player 2, 3, 4 or 5 makes the field as large as possible
* The 2 attackers (players 9 and 11) exert pressure on the ball. If they do this well and the defender in possession cannot pass the ball forward or into the midfield, the defender can always play the ball back to the goalkeeper, who can then start the game again.
* One player is always free on the other side of the field
* The goalkeeper plays the ball to the free man
* If one of the defenders makes a well-timed forward run from the back into the midfield and one of his teammates plays the ball to him, the buildup is successful.

OBJECTIVE:
- To improve buildup play in the first phase between players 2, 3, 4 and 5 on the one hand and players 6 and 8 on the other
- To create a one-player numerical advantage in midfield when a defender pushes forward

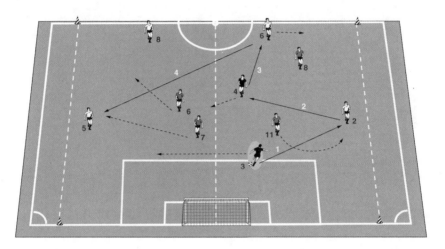

ORGANIZATION:
- 2 teams of 4 players with 2 neutral players
- The neutral players are always on the side of the team in possession
- In one zone, 4 play against 2
- In the other zone are 2 defenders
- When the ball is transferred to the left side they can defend
- Player 4 or 3 plays in front of the defense

INSTRUCTIONS:
- Coach with regard to time and space, for both defending and attacking
- Tactical positioning associated with each position
- For players 3 and 4, see the right moment and the space from behind the ball and play in front of the defense
- Shape of the team and distances between the players.
- Technical and tactical skills.

OBJECTIVE:
* To improve positional play

ORGANIZATION:
* Lay-off players can play 2-touch or 1-touch passes
* Try to retain possession
* The organization and shape of the team must be good
* 1 point is scored for 10 consecutive passes
* 1 point is scored when the third man is involved directly from a direct pass from a lay-off player

INSTRUCTIONS:
* The lay-off players should run on the balls of the feet with their knees slightly bent
* Face the ball. The lay-off players must exert pressure on the ball
* Passing and kicking technique
* Shape of the team must be good. The lay-off players must have the option of passing left, right, centrally and forward.
* The lay-off player in the middle and the midfielder must attune their movement to each other; with one moving toward the ball and the other staying away from it to give depth to the play.
* In midfield, move diagonally with respect to each other

OBJECTIVE:
* To improve positional play

ORGANIZATION:
* 3 groups of 4 players
* The lay-off players can play 2-touch or 1-touch passes
* The field measures 30 x 35 yards

INSTRUCTIONS:
* A lay-off player must not play the ball to another lay-off player
* Manner of playing the ball in
* Movement off the ball
* Shape of the team (organization)
* Communication

OBJECTIVE:
* To improve transition from attack to defense and vice versa when possession changes

ORGANIZATION:
* 4v4 on a field without goalkeepers (twice the size of the penalty area with handball goals)
* Score from free play or only directly or after receiving a pass
* A goal can only be scored when everyone has crossed the center line
* Play 4 periods of 4 minutes, then rest for 2 minutes

INSTRUCTIONS:
Attacking
* Circulate the ball quickly
* Encourage goalscoring capability
* Fast transition when possession changes
Defending
* Pressure your opponents
* Close up (make the field smaller)
* Take over an opponent (zone defending)
* Positional coaching

OBJECTIVE:
* To improve positional play using 2 small goals and 2 lines between the cones

ORGANIZATION:
* 2 teams play 4v4 on a relatively wide field
* One team defends the 2 small goals and tries to score by dribbling the ball over the line between two cones

INSTRUCTIONS:
* Keep the ball close to your foot and change direction frequently when dribbling
* Shield the ball with your body
* Look over the ball so that you can see where your teammates and opponents are
* Dribble into space and run fast with the ball
* Feint to the right and left
* After feinting, pass the ball, shoot or accelerate
* Feint with your body or by suddenly stopping and pretending to move in another direction, or by pretending that you are going to shoot or pass

OBJECTIVE:
• Speed of action, 1v1
• The run after the run
• To play in the third man

ORGANIZATION:
• Field measuring 16 x 32 yards
• 2 teams of 3 players
• 2 goalkeepers

INSTRUCTIONS:
• No goal kicks or corners
• If the third man scores (from a lay-off), this counts double
• The goalkeeper always starts the game
• The 4 lay-off players can play 1-touch or 2-touch passes
• Switch lay-off players after 3 minutes

OBJECTIVE:
* To improve speed of action
* The run after the run
* To play in the third man

ORGANIZATION:
* 2 teams of 4 players
* Each team has 1 lay-off player on each side of the goal
* Field measuring 32 x 20 yards
* Each team has its own coach
* 3 reps, each lasting 4 minutes

INSTRUCTIONS:
* The lay-off players must remain behind the line
* The lay-off players must pass the ball with their first touch
* If the ball goes out, the goalkeeper starts the game anew
* If a goal is scored by playing in the third man, this counts double

OBJECTIVE:
* Speed of action, 1v1
* The run after the run
* To play in the third man

ORGANIZATION:
* 2 teams of 4 players
* Each team has 1 lay-off player on each side of the field
* Field measuring 32 x 20 yards
* Each team has its own coach
* 3 repeats, each lasting 4 minutes

INSTRUCTIONS:
* When a team has possession, the first pass must be to a lay-off player
* The lay-off players must pass the ball with their first touch
* If the ball goes out, the goalkeeper starts the game anew
* Coach changes of pace
* If a goal is scored by playing in the third man, this counts double

OBJECTIVE:
- To improve (close) positional play for the purpose of playing the ball to the strikers

ORGANIZATION:
- In the central zone the teams play 4v4 after the coach plays the ball in from a random position
- The teams try to take the ball over the center line by means of close positional play and then to pass to the strikers
- Players can push up as they wish
- If the opposition wins possession, the game continues for just 15 seconds
- 2 new players then join the midfield (total of 20 field players)
- The free defender can push up in the defensive zone to create a 5v4 situation

INSTRUCTIONS:
- Look over the ball so you can see where your teammates and opponents are
- Dribble into space and run fast with the ball
- Try to play a combination whenever a teammate is free

OBJECTIVE:
- To create a scoring chance with a fast counterattack (maximum of 30 seconds) after a cross by the opposing team

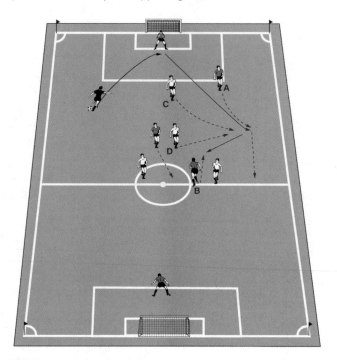

ORGANIZATION:
- 2 teams of 4 players plus goalkeepers
- The coach
- The field

INSTRUCTIONS:
- The players stand in their starting positions
- The coach or a player crosses the ball to the goalkeeper
- The goalkeeper throws the ball to player A, who is sprinting down the wing
- Players C and D try to pressure player A
- Player B drops off his marker and receives the ball from player A
- The players are free to choose the next moves (they must score within 30 seconds)
- Repeat 4 to 8 times
- Always return to the starting positions at a steady jogging pace

OBJECTIVE:
◆ To improve positional play

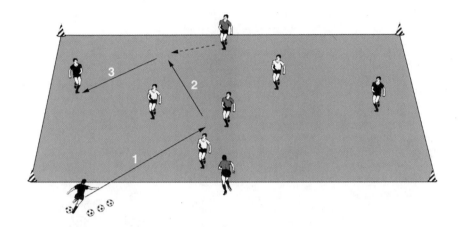

ORGANIZATION:
◆ A marked out field measuring 15 x 20 yards
◆ 2 teams of 3 players and 2 neutral players

INSTRUCTIONS:
◆ The coach plays the ball in
◆ The neutral players on the sides play with the team in possession
◆ After the team in possession loses the ball 3 times, it takes over the defending role

OBJECTIVE:
- To improve technique
- To carry out specific tasks
- To learn how to play under pressure

ORGANIZATION:
- Half field
- 8 players
- 1 goalkeeper
- 1 ball (10 extra balls)
- 10 to 20 repeats
- Practice for 10 to 15 minutes
- Player 7 from the opposing team exerts pressure from the right flank
- The task of player 10 is to make the field as large as possible by taking up position on the same flank as the ball and coming to meet the ball at the right moment
- If player 2, 3, 4 or 5 plays a 1-2 combination with player 10, the buildup is a success

OBJECTIVE:
* To improve technique
* To carry out specific tasks
* To learn how to play under pressure

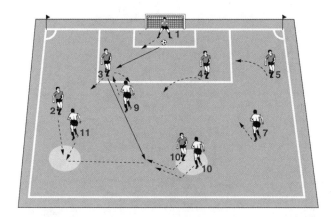

ORGANIZATION:
* Half field
* 9 players
* 1 goalkeeper
* 1 ball (10 extra balls)
* 10 to 20 repeats
* Practice for 10 to 15 minutes
* Player 10 from the opposing team moves infield
* He enters into a 1v1 duel
* Player 10 of the team in possession makes the field large, feints to make a run and then calls for the ball at the right moment
* If player 10 plays a 1-2 combination with player 2, 3, 4 or 5, the buildup is a success

INSTRUCTIONS:
* Correct the players and stop the game when a player chooses a wrong solution
* Show the players what their task is
* Show the defenders what they must do if one of them pushes up into midfield. Who covers his back?
* Show everyone how, depending on the situation, you can find space by moving 5 yards forward or backward
* Show how the attackers can exert pressure

OBJECTIVE:
+ To improve positional play
+ To learn how to play the ball in to the striker

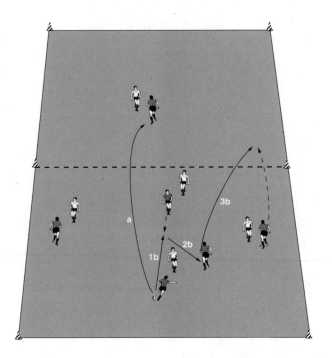

ORGANIZATION:
+ In a game of 5v4, using fast combination play to get the ball quickly to the striker
+ Or hit a long forward pass to the player running forward; do not dribble over the center line
+ Variation: the long forward pass can only be hit after 6 consecutive passes
+ Variation: Scoring in a goal

INSTRUCTIONS:
+ Play the ball firmly over the ground
+ Run into space
+ Ensure the team has a good shape
+ The striker drops back or makes a forward run at the right moment to receive the ball

OBJECTIVE:
• To improve transition from defense to attack and vice versa when possession changes

ORGANIZATION:
• Field the size of 2 penalty areas with 2 small goals at 1 end and a wider goal at the other end
• 2 teams: 4 defenders and a goalkeeper against 2 midfielders and 3 attackers
• Variation: the long forward pass can only be hit after 6 consecutive passes
• Play 3 x 4 minutes, then 2 minutes rest

INSTRUCTIONS:
Attacking
• Fast ball circulation
• Continue to play positionally

Defending
• Wait for the right moment to exert pressure
• The goalkeeper should participate in the field play and give instructions to the others
• Fast transition when possession changes
• Apply zonal marking

OBJECTIVE:
* To switch the play
* To use space
* To defend zonally
* To improve the shape of the team

ORGANIZATION:
* Half field
* 6 small goals formed by cones
* Free play or 1-touch or 2-touch play

INSTRUCTIONS:
* A point is scored by passing the ball between the cones to a teammate, who then touches the ball at least twice
* The ball must not be played higher than the height of the cones

SMALL SIDED GAMES (5V5)

OBJECTIVE:
* To switch the play
* To use space
* To defend zonally

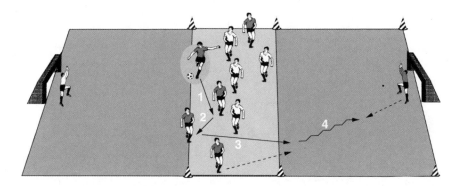

ORGANIZATION:
* 2 teams play 5v5 in the marked center zone
* Attacking zones are marked in front of each goal. The goals are defended by goalkeepers.
* Spare balls are placed beside each goal

INSTRUCTIONS:
* The game starts with 5v5 in the center zone
* The attackers pass the ball around, e.g. 5 times, then try to play a ball into the attacking zone for a player to run onto. The player must not enter the attacking zone before the ball. The attacker tries to score in the 1v1 situation with the goalkeeper.
* If the defenders win possession, the roles are swapped.
* After trying to score, the attacker runs back to the center zone and the coach sends the ball into play in the center zone again

OBJECTIVE:
* To switch the play
* To use space
* To defend zonally

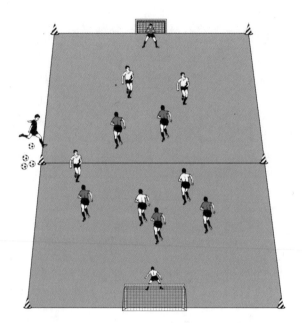

ORGANIZATION:
* 2 teams of 5 players
* 4 x 5 minutes
* Field 60 to 40 yards long
* 2 goals with goalkeepers
* Cones on the center line
* Coach stands on the sideline with a supply of balls

INSTRUCTIONS:
* Small sided game of 5v5 with 2 full sized goals defended by goalkeepers
* The team in possession tries to score using combination play
* If the ball goes out of play (over the side line or the end line), the coach immediately sends another ball into play.
* If the defenders win possession, they try to score
* As a variation, restrict the number of ball contacts in a team's own half

OBJECTIVE:
* To switch the play
* To use space
* To defend zonally

ORGANIZATION:
* 2 teams of 5 players and 2 neutral players
* 4 x 5 minutes
* Field 60 to 40 yards long
* 2 goal with goalkeeper and 2 small goals at each end
* Cones on the center line
* Coach stands on the sideline with a supply of balls

INSTRUCTIONS:
* Small sided game of 5v5 with 2 neutral players
* The team in possession tries to score in the full sized goal or 1 of the 2 small goals using combination play
* The 2 neutral players play with the team that has possession
* The team in possession must score within 1 minute
* If the ball goes out of play (over the side line or the end line), the coach immediately sends another ball into play.
* As a variation, restrict the number of ball contacts in a team's own half

OBJECTIVE:
* Playing a long ball forward after build-up play

ORGANIZATION:
* Field measuring 25 x 40 yards
* 3v3 with 4 neutral players (6v3) in zone A
* After 5 passes, the ball can be played forward to the neutral player in zone B
* Everyone moves into zone B, except 1 neutral player who stays in zone A
* Each forward pass into the other zone scores 1 point

INSTRUCTIONS:
* Contact between the passer and the player in the other zone
* Choosing the right moment to play the long ball forward
* The other players must push up quickly after the ball has been played forward
* Technical skills (controlling the ball, passing, kicking with the instep)

OBJECTIVE:
* The team of 6 tries to retain possession for as long as possible
* The team of 3 tries to win possession

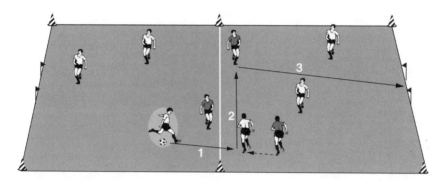

ORGANIZATION:
* Marked out field measuring 20 x 30 yards
* 1 small goal at each end
* 1 team of 6 players and 1 team of 3 players

INSTRUCTIONS:
* The 6 players are in possession and try to remain in possession for as long as possible, playing 1-touch or 2-touch passes.
* If the defenders win possession, they try to score in one of the 2 small goals
* After each 5-minute session and an active recuperation pause, 3 other players become defenders.
* Which group of defenders scores the most goals?

* To improve positional play

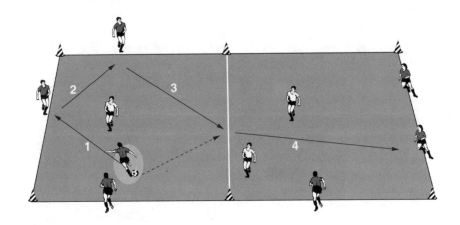

ORGANIZATION:
* Marked out field measuring 15 x 20 yards
* 6 players around the edge of the field and 1 player on the field
* 3 defenders

INSTRUCTIONS:
* The 6 players around the edge of the field and their teammate on the field try to remain in possession as long as possible.
* The players around the edge of the field can pass the ball with first or second touch and pass to the player on the field as often as possible
* The 3 defenders try to win possession and then play 3v1, trying to retain possession as long as possible with 1-touch passes

OBJECTIVE:
- To improve positional play

ORGANIZATION:
- Field measuring 25 x 40 yards
- 2 teams of 4 players
- The team in possession has 2 other players (lay-off players)

INSTRUCTIONS:
- 1 lay-off player stands at each end of the field and has to play 1-touch passes
- After the defenders win the ball 3 times the players switch roles

OBJECTIVE:
- To improve first-phase buildup play between players 2, 3, 4 and 5 on the one hand and players 6 and 8 on the other
- Creating an extra man in midfield by pushing up a free defender

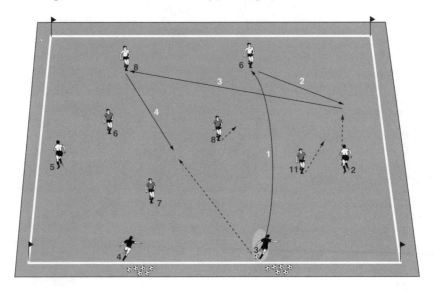

ORGANIZATION:
- 2 teams of 4 players and 2 neutral players
- The neutral players always play with the team in possession
- Assign the players to their specific positions. The 2 central defenders are the neutral players.
- This drill is the same as the previous one, except that it takes place in a rectangle rather than 2 zones
- The game is always restarted by player 3 or 4, who start off alongside each other and choose the right moment to move into midfield.

INSTRUCTIONS:
- Coach with regard to time and space, for both defending and attacking
- Tactical positioning associated with each position
- For players 3 and 4, see the right moment and the space from behind the ball and play in front of the defense
- Shape of the team and distances between the players.
- Technical and tactical skills.

OBJECTIVE:
* Passing accurately to the striker over the ground

ORGANIZATION:
* Half field
* Minimum of 12 players

INSTRUCTIONS:
* Small sided game of 6v5 (plus goalkeeper)
* Team of 6: Striker can play as he likes, while the others have to play the ball with their first or second touch. If the ball goes above hip height, the opposition gets a free kick
* Team of 5: Try to score in one of the small goals
* Focus: How can 5 players put pressure on 6 opponents

OBJECTIVE:
* To improve positional play

ORGANIZATION:
* Try to retain possession and play the ball to the goalkeeper on the end line
* The goalkeeper plays the ball to the team that passed it to him
* Playing the ball to the goalkeeper scores 1 point
* You can play the ball 2 or more times in sequence to the goalkeeper, but this does not gain you any more points
* Free play, maximum of 3 touches or maximum of 2 touches

OBJECTIVE:
* To improve positional play by creating lots of scoring chances

ORGANIZATION:
* 2 teams of 6 players
* 4 x 5 minutes
* Field 50 to 30 yards long
* 2 goals on each end line and each side line

INSTRUCTIONS:
* Small sided game of 6v6 with 8 small goals
* The team in possession can score in one of the opposition's 4 goals
* Defenders exert pressure on the side of the field where the ball is
* Defenders must communicate with each other
* Fast transition from defense to attack and vice versa when possession changes

OBJECTIVE:
* To improve first-phase buildup play between players 2, 3, 4 and 5 on the one hand and players 6 and 8 on the other
* Creating an extra man in midfield by pushing up a free defender

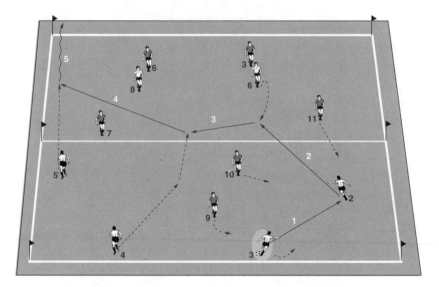

ORGANIZATION:
* 2 teams of 6 players
* Assign the players to their specific positions.
* A goal is scored by dribbling over the opposition's end line
* In step 1, players 7 and 11 and players 2 and 5 should not try to pressure their opponents after losing possession, but allow the opposition to have a 4v2 numerical advantage in its buildup play.
* In step 2, free play is allowed

INSTRUCTIONS:
* Tactical positioning associated with each position
* For players 3 and 4, seeing the right moment and the space from behind the ball and playing in front of the defense
* Shape of the team and distances between the players. Play the ball forward rather than square, but remember that the priority is on retaining possession.
* Technical and tactical skills.
* When defending, cooperation between the last line and the midfield with regard to player 10.

OBJECTIVE:
* To encourage buildup play out of defense

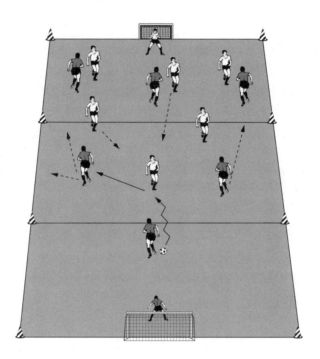

ORGANIZATION:
* 2 teams of 6 players, with goalkeepers
* Rectangular field, divided into 3 zones.
* The size of field depends on the size of the group
* Various goals (large, small, 4 in all)

INSTRUCTIONS:
* If a goal is scored after buildup play out of defense, 1 point is awarded
* If a goal is scored after winning the ball in midfield, 2 points are awarded
* If a goal is scored after winning the ball in the opposition's defensive zone, 3 points are awarded

OBJECTIVE:
◆ To improve buildup play

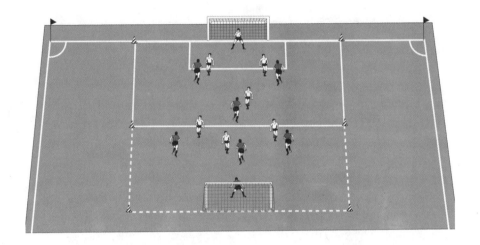

ORGANIZATION:
◆ Field the size of 2 penalty areas
◆ If the ball goes out of play, the goalkeeper immediately sends a new ball into play.

INSTRUCTIONS:
◆ 2-touch play. The first touch must control the ball, so that the ball can be passed with the second touch.
◆ As a variation, a maximum of 2 touches can be allowed.
◆ As a variation, only 1 touch can be allowed.

OBJECTIVE:

Defenders:
* To put pressure on the ball as quickly as possible
* To close down space around the ball
* To win the ball and score after good buildup play

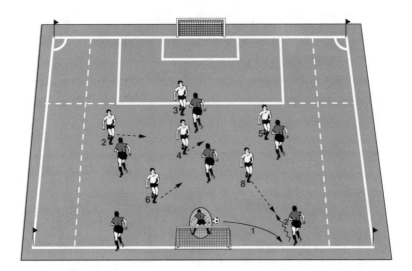

ORGANIZATION:
* The goalkeeper starts the buildup on the right or left
* Defenders try to score in the goal defended by the goalkeeper
* The attackers can score in the empty goal after the ball has been played to an attacker in the penalty area
* The defenders can also defend in the penalty area

INSTRUCTIONS:
* The player closest to the ball puts pressure on the ball (8).
* The players around the ball mark their opponents closely (3, 4 and 5).
* The other players close down space by moving closer together and moving infield (6 and 2).
* The players with an overall view of the play communicate with the others (2 and 3)
* The defenders choose the right moment to win the ball

OBJECTIVE:
* To play in the third man

ORGANIZATION:
* 2 teams of 6 players
* 1-3-1-2 formation
* A goal can only be scored after playing in the third man
* Free play, but a goal scored by the third man after a lay-off by one of the 2 strikers counts double

INSTRUCTIONS:
* Play 4 x 5 minutes
* The strikers must create space so that their teammates can pass to them.
* Correct timing of pass.
* Cooperation between the strikers
* Communication between the players

OBJECTIVE:
* To improve positional play

ORGANIZATION:
* A marked out grid measuring 15 x 20 yards
* 3 teams of 3 players and 1 neutral player

INSTRUCTIONS:
* The coach starts the play by passing to the neutral player
* The players on the side lines must play the ball with their first touch
* After possession has been lost 3 times, the next team defends

OBJECTIVE:
+ To improve positional play

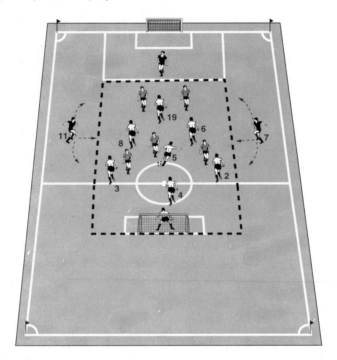

ORGANIZATION:
+ The 7 players score by shooting into the empty goal after a lay-off by player 9
+ The players in the team of 7 are only allowed 2 touches each time they receive the ball
+ The team of 5 tries to score in the goal defended by the goalkeeper
+ The players in the team of 5 can play as they wish
+ The zones for the lay-off players are free. The lay-off players must pass with their first touch
+ The goalkeeper joins in the buildup play of the team of 7.

INSTRUCTIONS:
+ Familiarization with coaching terms
+ Short combinations, 1-2 combinations
+ Learning how to play in a given formation
+ Emphasis on taking up good positions

SMALL SIDED GAMES (7V3)

OBJECTIVE:
* To improve positional play

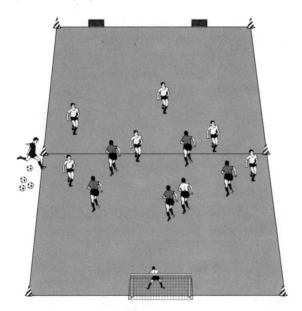

ORGANIZATION:
* 4 x 5 minutes
* Field 60 to 40 yards long
* 1 full size goal, defended by a goalkeeper, and 2 small goals on the other end line
* Cones at each end of the center line
* Coach stands on side line with supply of balls.

INSTRUCTIONS:
* 7v5
* The team in possession tries to score in the full size goal within 30 seconds, otherwise the coach sends another ball into play from the side-line
* The team of 5 tries to score in the small goals
* Each time the ball goes out of play (over the end lines or the side lines) the coach immediately sends another ball into play
* The players in the team of 7 can only touch the ball twice each time they receive it

OBJECTIVE:
* To improve positional play

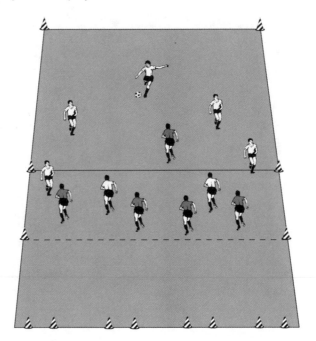

ORGANIZATION:
* 12 players
* 4 x 5 minutes
* Field 50 to 30 yards long
* 4 goals on one end line (at least 2 yards wide)
* Cones 15 from this end line

INSTRUCTIONS:
* 7v5
* The team of 7 can score in 1 of the 4 goals from the marked zone, but only from a direct pass
* The team of 5 can score by dribbling the ball over the end line
* Defenders must communicate
* Variation: Defend 3 small goals

OBJECTIVE:
* To improve positional play

ORGANIZATION:
* 13 field players and 1 goalkeeper
* 3 x 7 minutes
* Field 50 to 65 yards long
* 1 full size goal defended by a goalkeeper
* Cones on the center line

INSTRUCTIONS:
* 7v6 with 1 full size goal
* The team of 7 attacks the goal
* If the ball is won in the opposition's half and a goal is then scored, the goal counts double
* Defenders must communicate
* The team of 5 can score by dribbling over the center line

OBJECTIVE:
* To improve positional play

ORGANIZATION:
* The team of 6 tries to pressure the opposition in the marked zone
* The team of 6 scores by dribbling the ball over the line
* The team of 7 tries to score in the goal

INSTRUCTIONS:
* Try to build up moves while retaining possession
* Put pressure on the ball when the player in possession is on the flank

OBJECTIVE:
* To improve positional play

ORGANIZATION:
* The size of the field depends on the level of skill of the players
* Each goal is defended by a goalkeeper
* A team of 6 players plays against a team of 7 players

INSTRUCTIONS:
* The team of 6 tries to exert pressure by standing off the opponent
* Close down space around the ball and make the field narrower
* Exert pressure on the flanks
* Force the player in possession to play a long ball forward
* Close off the center

OBJECTIVE:
* To improve buildup play toward the strikers
* To improve the transition from defense to attack and vice versa when possession changes

ORGANIZATION:
* Full field
* 2 teams of 9 players and 2 goalkeepers
* The team of 7 tries to play the ball to its strikers from out of its own half

INSTRUCTIONS:
* The 7 players (in the half where 7 are playing against 6) try to retain possession with the aim of reaching their strikers with a pass
* If the 6 players (in the half where 7 are playing against 6) or the 3 players (in the half where 3 are playing against 2) win possession, they have 20 seconds to score from a counter attack
* The attacking zone can also be reached by passing to an advancing midfielder (who is not allowed to enter the attacking zone before the ball crosses the center line)

OBJECTIVE:
* To improve positional play in the attacking phase when in possession
* To practice attacking combinations to create scoring chances

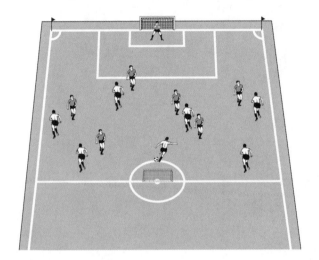

ORGANIZATION:
* Team of 7 can play freely
* Limit the number of ball contacts in midfield
* Free attacking play
* Competitive game in which the team of 6 can score in the small goal on the center line

INSTRUCTIONS:
* Players 7 and 11 face the ball, with their back to the side line, to receive a pass, so that they can play the ball forward
* Encourage players 7 and 11 to make individual runs
* Try to make a long forward pass from the midfield as soon as possible, after which a midfielder (third man) links up
* Player 9 must start as far forward as possible and move out to the flanks
* If a pass is on, player 10 must run into the space left by player 9 when player 9 moves toward the flank
* Players 6 and 8 must stand diagonally behind players 7 and 11 when the latter are in possession of the ball
* If the play is switched, 6 and 8 can also push forward
* If player 6 or 8 has the ball, player 4 must be behind the ball in order to switch flanks

OBJECTIVE:
* To improve positional play

ORGANIZATION:
* Free positional play, touching the ball a maximum of 2 or 3 times
* The team in possession plays the ball to the goalkeeper in his zone and the players run into space to receive the ball
* A pass to the goalkeeper scores 1 point. Another point can only be scored after the ball has been played to the other goalkeeper.
* A goalkeeper can be involved several times in the buildup play
* The players must not enter the goalkeeper's zone

INSTRUCTIONS:
In possession
* Take up position to receive a pass, run into space, pass to another player so that he can play the ball to the goalkeeper.
On losing possession
* Exert pressure on the ball, prevent (long) pass to goalkeeper (important in order to prevent a counter attack)

OBJECTIVE:
• To improve positional play

ORGANIZATION:
• The 4 neutral players stand between the cones
• Play 7v7 in the field
• The neutral players may not touch the ball more than twice each time it is played to them
• The players in midfield can play freely
• The emphasis is on moving out toward the lay-off players, overlapping and linking up

OBJECTIVE:
* To improve positional play

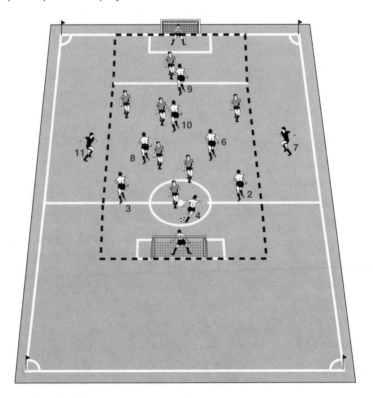

ORGANIZATION:
* A goal counts as 1 point
* A goal from a cross counts as 2 points
* The wingers can only touch the ball 2 times whenever they receive it

INSTRUCTIONS:
* Coaching
* Controlling a pass, crossing, finishing
* Playing in a formation with wingers
* Encouraging wing play
* Choosing position in front of goal
* Transition from attack to defense after losing possession. Picking up rebounds.

OBJECTIVE:
* To improve transition from defense to attack and vice versa when possession changes

ORGANIZATION:
* Field measuring 40 x 60 yards, with a marked zone at each end
* 2 teams of 7 players
* 2 neutral players

INSTRUCTIONS:
* The team in possession can score by dribbling into the zone or passing to a player in the zone
* If a team scores, it remains in possession
* The ball must cross the center line before another goal can be scored
* The 2 neutral players always play with the team in possession, but cannot score

OBJECTIVE:
* To improve the transition from defense to attack and vice versa when possession changes

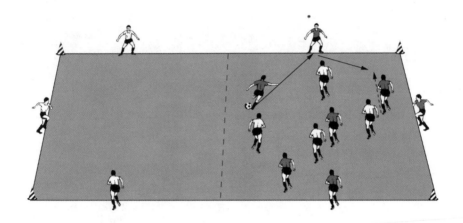

ORGANIZATION:
* 2 teams of 7 players distributed over 2 zones

INSTRUCTIONS:
* In one zone the players play 4v4 or 5v5. The team in possession has 3 lay-off players.
* If the other team wins the ball, the players hit a long ball to one of their lay-off players
* Both teams move into the other zone; only the lay-off players stay where they are
* Change of task/team after a few minutes

OBJECTIVE:
◆ To improve positional play

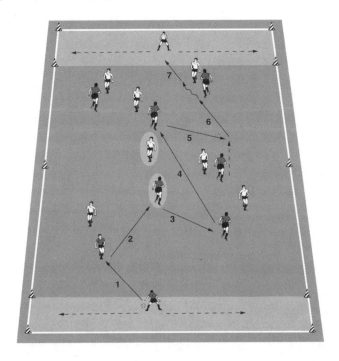

ORGANIZATION:
◆ The buildup play starts with the goalkeeper, who plays the ball to one of his 7 teammates.
◆ If this player cannot pass square or forward, he can play the ball back to the goalkeeper.
◆ If the ball crosses the end line where the opposition's goalkeeper is positioned, this counts for 1 point.

INSTRUCTIONS:
◆ Communicate with players who are less than 5 yards from an opponent
◆ Give a warning when an opponent is behind a teammate
◆ Do not just make runs toward the ball. Make runs away from the ball to create space.
◆ Alternate between short triangular passing combinations and 1-2 combinations followed by a long ball over the ground or through the air

OBJECTIVE:
* To improve combination play between the central defender, the 4 midfielders and the 2 strikers with the aim of scoring

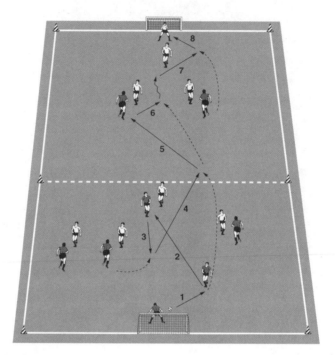

ORGANIZATION:
* 5 defenders against 4 attackers in the buildup zone, with one of the five players pushing up into the attacking zone to create a 3v3 situation and help to score.

INSTRUCTIONS:
* Improving positional play over short and long distances by combination play and good buildup and cooperation, while avoiding losing possession during the buildup
* It is important for the two strikers to call for the ball at the right moment. One striker runs toward the ball and the other runs forward and wide, forcing the two defenders to follow
* The whole team must link up well in the final phase
* The opposing team can also score. The buildup then starts at the other end.

OBJECTIVE:
* To improve ball control and speed of reaction in tight situations

ORGANIZATION:
* Half field
* 2 teams of 7 players plus 2 neutral goalkeepers

INSTRUCTIONS:
* Game of 7v7 with 2 neutral goalkeepers who can chose position as they wish
* Free play when in possession, or maximum of 3 touches each time a player receives the ball
* A team can score a point by passing directly to one of the two goalkeepers, provided the goalkeeper catches the ball

OBJECTIVE:

* To circulate the ball rapidly in tight situations, find the free man and switch the play.

ORGANIZATION:

* Half field with free center zone measuring 15 x 15 yards
* 2 teams of 7 players plus 2 neutral players

INSTRUCTIONS:

* Only the 2 neutral players can enter the center zone
* Free play when in possession, or maximum of 3 touches each time a player receives the ball
* A team can score a point if a pass from the center zone results in the third man being played in
* Additional focus: Cooperation between the 4 midfielders and the 3 strikers

OBJECTIVE:
- To retain possession and to try to play the ball as far forward as possible
- To improve cooperation between the lines and specific moments per position when in possession, so that the players can find each other more easily during a game (routine)

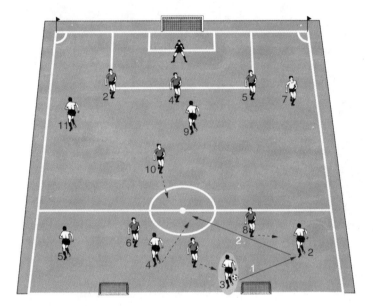

ORGANIZATION:
- 4v3 in the buildup play
- Retain possession in a controlled manner
- Play the ball forward at the right moment

INSTRUCTIONS:
- Coach with regard to time and space, for both defending and attacking
- Tactical positioning associated with each position
- The fullback, for example
- Facing the ball. When, and up to where, to support the right midfielder or striker
- Playing the ball through the center
- Never play alongside or behind each other
- Distance between players in different positions
- Shape of the team

OBJECTIVE:
* To improve positional play

ORGANIZATION:
* Free play or 2 ball contacts
* Field measuring 20 x 30 yards
* Learn instructions for communication on the field (Now! Turn! Lay it off! Hold it! etc.)
* Learn technical aspects (good ball circulation, conditions, ball speed, passing to the correct foot, controlling the ball, etc.)
* Stop the game when possession changes (to coach the players about the situation and make changes)
* Progress from the buildup toward switching from attack to defense and vice versa

OBJECTIVE:
* To learn to retain possession for as long as possible
* To switch quickly from defense to attack and vice versa when possession changes

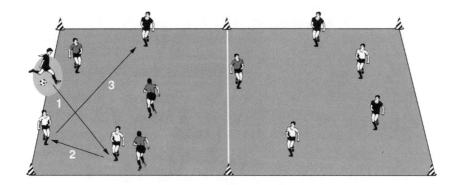

ORGANIZATION:
* Field measuring 25 x 35 yards
* 3 teams of 4 players

INSTRUCTIONS:
* Two teams work together as attackers, resulting in 8v4, and try to stay in possession as long as possible
* When the attackers lose the ball, the defenders become attackers and the team that caused the ball to be lost takes over the defensive role
* The attacking and defending teams thus change roles continuously
* The players continuously switch from attacking to defending and vice versa

OBJECTIVE:
* To improve positional play

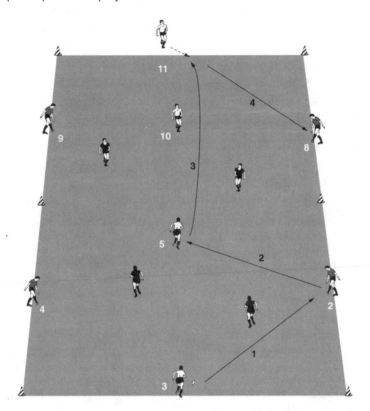

ORGANIZATION:
* The size of the field depends on the level of skill of the players
* 3 teams of 4 players

INSTRUCTIONS:
* Players 3, 5, 10 and 11 (the central axis of the team) form the team that is in possession
* The lay-off players always play with the team that is in possession
* When the defenders win the ball, the lay-off players and the defenders switch roles
* The players in the central axis thus always remain in their positions

OBJECTIVE:
* To learn how to exert pressure collectively

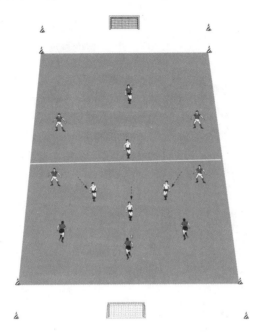

ORGANIZATION:
* Field: Width 20 to 25 yards, length 30 to 35 yards
* 8 players try to retain possession
* 4 defenders try to win possession; if they do so they can score in one of the goals.
* The defenders adopt a diamond formation. The player closest to the ball pressures the player in possession and must avoid being passed.
* 2 defenders cover his back on either side

INSTRUCTIONS:
Attacking
* Controlled ball circulation
* Stay in position

Defending
* Be on the alert for the right moment to exert pressure
* Switch quickly from defense to attack after winning possession

OBJECTIVE:
* To retain possession of the ball and circulate it quickly
* To improve cooperation between the lines

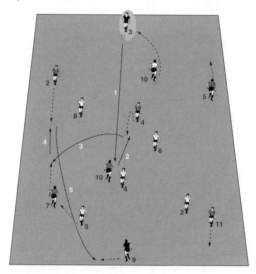

ORGANIZATION:
* 2 teams of 6 players with 2 neutral players
* The neutral players always play with the team in possession
* Size of field depends on age and level of players, but should not be too narrow (25 to 40 yards). This has to do with the central position of players 4 and 10.
* The main priority is to assign the players to specific positions.
* When possession is lost, the players must communicate in order to be able to defend zonally

INSTRUCTIONS:
General
* If possible, pass forward rather than square (and to the correct foot)
* Choose a good position - do not stand in line with an opponent.
* Choose the right moment to take up a position (run toward the ball or create space or run into space)
* Play in the third man (triangular short-passing)
Specific
* Tactical positioning associated with each position. Face the ball.
* When passing in the central axis, do not play the ball to the side of or behind the target player

OBJECTIVE:
* To improve the buildup play of the goalkeeper and 4 defenders under pressure from the 3 strikers of the opposing team

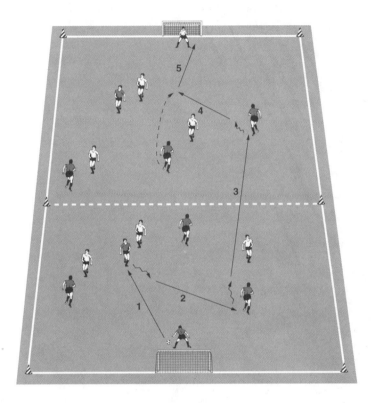

ORGANIZATION:
* 4v3 in the buildup and attacking zones
* In progressing to the attacking zone, the ball must be played to one of the 4 midfielders against the resistance of 3 opponents
* The goalkeeper plays the ball in to one of the 2 central players or one of the 2 fullbacks

INSTRUCTIONS:
* Choose the correct moment to play the ball in
* Make runs away from and toward the ball

OBJECTIVE:
- To retain possession and try to play the ball as far forward as possible
- To improve cooperation between the lines and specific moments per position when in possession, so that the players can find each other more easily during a game (routine)

ORGANIZATION:
- 4v2 in the buildup play
- Retain possession in a controlled manner
- Play the ball forward at the right moment

INSTRUCTIONS:
- If possible, pass forward rather than square (but possession is the first priority)
- Play the ball to the correct foot, depending on the position of the opponent
- Choose a good position - do not stand in line with an opponent.
- Choose the right moment to take up a position (run toward the ball or create space or run into space)
- Technical skills (ball control, use of the ball, speed of reaction, etc.)
- Tactical skills (overview of the situation in the final third, forward passing, anticipation of situation)
- Play in the third man (triangular short-passing)

OBJECTIVE:
* To improve positional play when in possession in the buildup phase
* To improve the ability to play the ball forward, especially the first pass after winning possession

ORGANIZATION:
* Two-thirds field, with 2 goals
* Maximum of 3 ball contacts in own half, free play in attacking half
* 7 and 11 only join in when the team has possession
* 7 and 11 can attempt to disrupt the opposition's buildup in the opposition's half
* 7 and 11 play a full part, so that a game of 8v8 ensues.

INSTRUCTIONS:
* Perfect positional play when in possession (basic task): 7 and 11 start on the side line and stand facing the ball; 9 stands as far forward as possible; 3 or 4 pushes through continuously to provide support; 2 and 5 stand ready to receive a crossfield pass
* After winning possession, the first pass should be forward, if possible
* Make forward runs after gaining possession and passing forward (third man links up)
* Encourage players 7 and 11 to enter into 1v1 duels followed by a cross
* Play the ball in cleanly at the right pace
* Positions in front of goal for a cross

OBJECTIVE:
* Practice exerting pressure

ORGANIZATION:
* Half field
* Positional game of 8v7 or 6v7 with 1 goalkeeper

INSTRUCTIONS:
* Pressure the opposition when in possession and when trying to regain possession
* The team with a numerical advantage can score
* The team with a numerical disadvantage and the goalkeeper try to prevent goals from being scored and play to gain possession and slow the tempo
* Switch after 3 minutes

OBJECTIVE:
* To improve buildup play out of the attacking team's own half, with the priority on cooperating to enable a long forward pass to be made

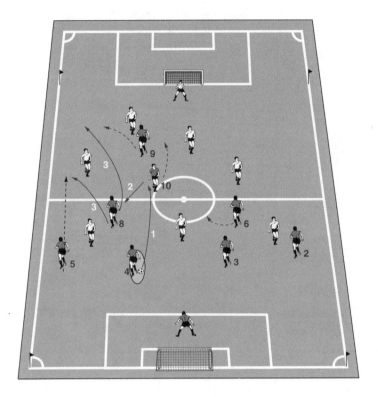

ORGANIZATION:
* Own half to the penalty area

INSTRUCTIONS:
* Weighting of the pass, kicking with the instep, controlling the ball
* Maintaining shape of team (distances between players); timing of the forward pass (communication)
* Non-verbal communication by means of runs off the ball. Verbal communication to indicate where the ball should be played. Coordination of runs by players 10 and 9.

OBJECTIVE:
* To improve positional play

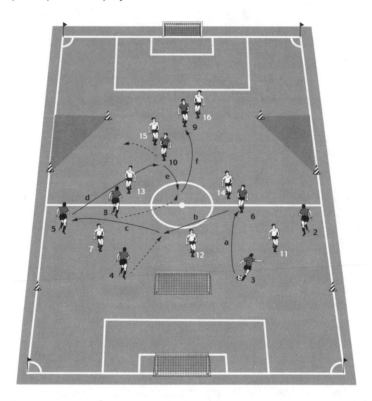

ORGANIZATION:
* Players 6 and 8 are not allowed to enter the dark-shaded triangles behind the cones (no relation to real match conditions)
* Expansion with goalkeeper
* The game is always started by player 3 or 4

INSTRUCTIONS:
* Practice specific variants in the buildup play two or three times
* The players then decide themselves which variant will be played
* The coach gives instructions to the opposition, such as "Play more on the flank," etc.

OBJECTIVE:
* To improve positional play

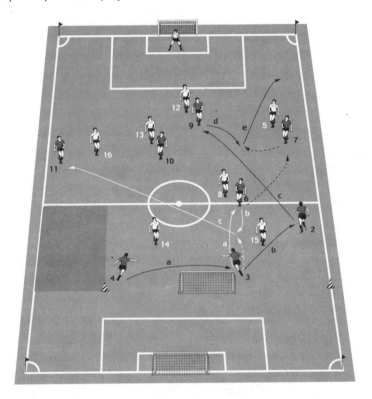

ORGANIZATION:
* Three-quarter field. Players may not enter the dark-shaded rectangle.
* Expansion to 8v8 with goalkeepers or 7v7 with goalkeepers
* The game is first practiced over the right flank, then over the left

INSTRUCTIONS:
* Practice specific variants in the buildup play two or three times
* The players then decide themselves which variant will be played
* The coach gives instructions to the opposition, such as "Play more on the flank," etc.

OBJECTIVE:
- To avoid being kicked, to think in advance and to react quickly

ORGANIZATION:
- Field the size of the penalty area
- If the ball goes out of play, the goalkeeper immediately sends a new ball into play.
- Collect the balls during the break for recuperation
- Quick change of goalkeeper after each game

INSTRUCTIONS:
- Keep the field as wide as possible
- Careful build-up to a cross
- Make sure that the cross is executed technically correctly

OBJECTIVE:

To improve buildup play, with the emphasis on

- exploiting 'third-man situations' (1-touch finishing)
- fast reactions (2-touch play in the buildup, 1-touch finishing)
- switching the play when under pressure

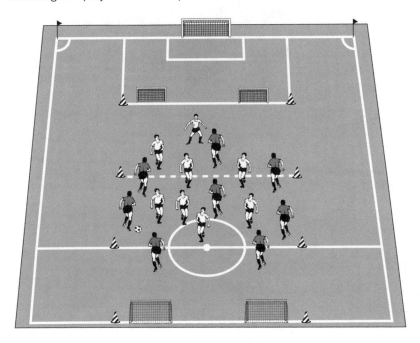

ORGANIZATION:

- Field measuring 60 x 40 yards, divided into 3 zones (15, 30 and 15 yards)
- 2 small goals at each end

INSTRUCTIONS:

- Free play in the central zone (series 1 and 2) then 2-touch play (series 3 and 4)
- Free play in the attacking zones, but 1-touch finishing
- 4 series of 8 minutes

OBJECTIVE:
- To improve the transition from defense to attack and vice versa when possession changes

ORGANIZATION:
- 2 teams of 8 players with goalkeepers in marked zones
- After 5 ball contacts, the team in possession tries to pass to an unmarked player
- The unmarked player hits a long pass to the goalkeeper in the other zone
- The team without the ball must try to prevent the long pass by exerting pressure
- A time limit can also be introduced

INSTRUCTIONS:

Attacking
- Fast ball circulation
- Be sure the team keeps its shape

Defending
- Wait for the right moment to exert pressure
- Fast transition from defense to attack after winning possession

OBJECTIVE:
* To improve the transition from defense to attack and vice versa when possession changes

ORGANIZATION:
* 2 teams of 8 players with goalkeepers
* The goalkeeper of one team acts as a sweeper
* The other team can score by hitting a long ball into the empty goal
* The team with the sweeper tries to exert pressure (defending a long away from its own goal) in such a way that the team in possession cannot hit such a long ball
* After 7 minutes the teams swap roles

INSTRUCTIONS:
Attacking
* Fast ball circulation
* Be sure the team keeps its shape

Defending
* Wait for the right moment to exert pressure
* Participation and communication by the goalkeeper.
* Fast transition from defense to attack after winning possession

OBJECTIVE:
• To learn to play on a 1-3-2-3 formation (plus a neutral player)

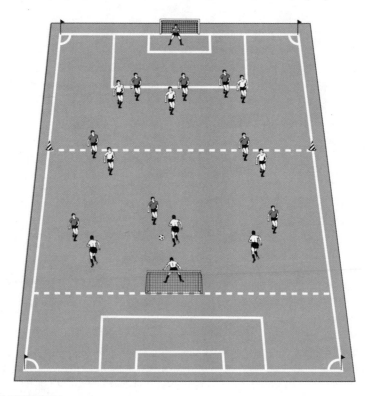

ORGANIZATION:
• Three-quarter field
• Free play; the neutral player is allowed 2 ball contacts each time he receives a pass
• A goal is only valid if the neutral player is in the opposition's half

INSTRUCTIONS:
• Neutral player must switch the play
• Choose position of neutral player
• Exploit numerical superiority
• Transition from defense to attack: Neutral player must be in a position to receive a direct pass and must call for the ball

OBJECTIVE:

• To create a scoring chance against a 5-strong zonal defense

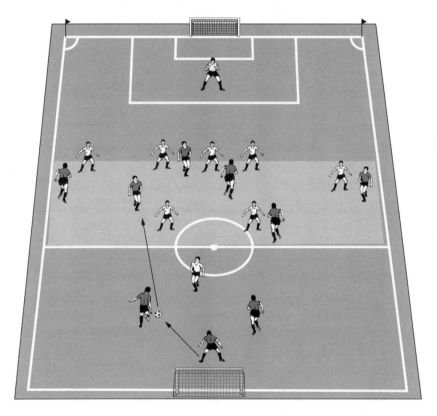

ORGANIZATION:

• 2 teams of 8 players [+ goalkeeper]
• 6 attackers play against 7 defenders in the marked zone
• The two central defenders play a supporting role in their own half, against the resistance of a striker who puts them under pressure

INSTRUCTIONS:

• Midfielders must make lots of runs
• Flank players must keep the field wide and feint to make runs
• Strikers must alternate in calling for the ball

OBJECTIVE:
- Full field with an enlarged area where the goalkeeper can operate

ORGANIZATION:
- Build-up out of defense
- Preventing long ball forward
- Constant pressure on player in possession

INSTRUCTIONS:
- You can score a point by playing the ball through the air into the hands of your own goalkeeper
- 1-touch play only

OBJECTIVE:
* Positional game to improve the cooperation between the strikers and the midfielders so that midfielders can get into dangerous positions in front of goal more often.

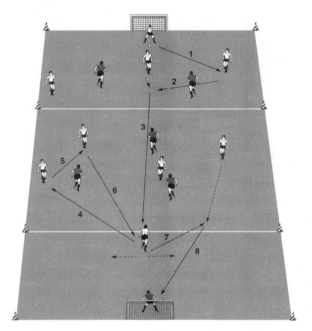

ORGANIZATION:
* Field measuring 45 x 35 yards
* 9v5 with 2 goalkeepers. The coach focuses on the team of 9.
* The team of 9 must play 1-touch or 2-touch soccer
* The team of 9 must get the ball forward to the striker as quickly as possible during the buildup and then get its midfielders into scoring positions.
* If the defenders intercept the ball, they must try to score out of free play within 30 seconds, otherwise the team of 9 can start another buildup.

INSTRUCTIONS:
* Communication between the players in the buildup move and the striker
* Play the ball to the correct foot (fast ball circulation)
* Shape of the team and involvement of the wingers
* Timing of the linkup by the midfielders

OBJECTIVE:
- To retain possession, trying to play the ball as far forward as possible
- To improve cooperation between the lines; specific moments per position when in possession, so that the players can find each other more easily during a game (routine)

ORGANIZATION:
- 9v6 in the buildup play, with the goalkeeper at one end and the striker (9) at the other.
- When the team of 9 loses possession, the teams play 7v7 with the striker (9) joining in at the back as the seventh player

INSTRUCTIONS:
- If possible, pass forward rather than square (but possession is the first priority)
- Play the ball to the correct foot, depending on the position of the opponent
- Choose a good position - do not stand in line with an opponent.
- Choose the right moment to take up a position (run toward the ball or create space or run into space)
- Technical skills (ball control, use of the ball, speed of reaction, etc.)
- Tactical skills (overview of the situation in the final third, forward passing, anticipation of situation)
- Play in the third man (triangular short-passing)

OBJECTIVE:

Team that does not have the ball
- To pressure the opposition and push the opposition players toward the side of the field (where there is less space).

Team in possession
- To escape the pressure by playing a crossfield pass (free player should be available to receive a pass at the back)

ORGANIZATION:
- 2 teams of 9 players
- Field 45 to 50 yards long (straddling the center line) over the full width

INSTRUCTIONS:
- 4 series of 3 minutes (playing time) then 2-minute break for recuperation
- 1-touch or 2-touch play in the buildup. Free play in the attacking zone.
- A goal is scored by dribbling the ball over the end line

OBJECTIVE:

Team that does not have the ball
- To pressure the opposition and push the opposition players toward the side of the field (where there is less space).

Team in possession
- To escape the pressure by playing a crossfield pass (free player should be available to receive a pass at the back)

ORGANIZATION:
- 2 teams of 9 players and 2 goalkeepers
- Field 45 to 50 yards long (straddling the center line) over the full width

INSTRUCTIONS:
- Free play in a 1-3-3-2 formation
- Series until 2-0 or 2-1; total 25 minutes
- Losers do 15 press-ups

OBJECTIVE:

* To choose the right moment to play the ball to the players in the following zone

ORGANIZATION:

* Three quarter field divided into 3 zones

INSTRUCTIONS:

* The game starts in the first zone with 4v4
* The team in possession waits for the right moment to play the ball forward to the 2 teammates in the center zone. At that moment one player from each team pushes in the first zone pushes up into the center zone
* There is a 3v3 situation in the center zone, although the original 2 players may decide to exploit the 2v2 situation very quickly.
* Finally the ball is played to the 3 players in the attacking zone

OBJECTIVE:
* To remain in possession for as long as possible
* To switch quickly from attack to defense and vice versa when possession changes

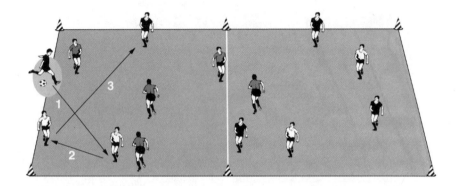

ORGANIZATION:
* Marked field measuring 30 x 40 yards
* 2 teams of 5 players and one team of 4 players

INSTRUCTIONS:
* 2 teams work together as attackers, trying to stay in possession as long as possible
* When the attackers lose the ball, the defenders become attackers and the team that caused the ball to be lost takes over the defensive role
* The situation changes constantly: If the team of 4 forms the defense there is a 10v4 situation, and if the team of 4 is in the attack, there is a 9v5 situation.

OBJECTIVE:
* To improve the transition from attack to defense and vice versa when possession changes

ORGANIZATION:
* Field measuring 30 x 30 yards
* 3 teams
* 4 goals

INSTRUCTIONS:
* Choose the correct moment to exert pressure on the player in possession
* Exert pressure whenever a high ball is played
* Stand off a weaker player, enabling him to gain possession.
* The last man instructs his colleagues when they should put pressure on the player with the ball
* 5 players (in a diamond shape) exert pressure on the ball at the correct moments, while the other 10 players try to retain possession for 2 to 3 minutes

OBJECTIVE:
- To progress through game patterns to 10v8 in 3 zones

ORGANIZATION:
- Zone 1: 5v3 from fixed positions. The buildup starts with the goalkeeper, who plays the ball to player 3. The game then starts.
- Zone 2: 4v3 from fixed positions. Solutions depend on the positions of the defenders.
- Zone 3: The following players become involved: Number 11 crosses, number 9 at the near post, number 10 on the penalty spot, number 7 at the far post, numbers 6 and 8 on the edge of the penalty area and numbers 2 and 3 as defenders.

INSTRUCTIONS:
- The players must seek their own creative solutions

OBJECTIVE:
- To exploit a 3v2 situation
- To have an extra man in the buildup
- To score by dribbling over the end line

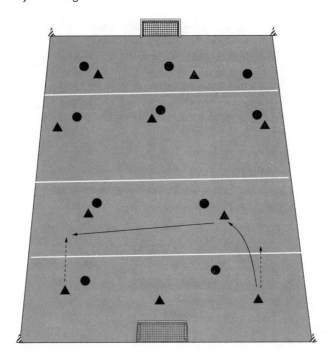

ORGANIZATION:
- 2 teams of 10 players
- In the defensive zone are 2 or 3 attackers and 2 or 3 defenders
- In the buildup, the ball is played to a player in the next zone and one player pushes up to create a numerical advantage.
- The fact that player has pushed up creates a 3v3 situation in the attacking zone
- In the final phase, play with large goals and goalkeepers (11v11)

INSTRUCTIONS:
- The midfield players must make lots of runs
- The flank players must stay on the flanks to keep the field wide, and feint to make runs
- The strikers take turns in calling for the ball

OBJECTIVE:
* To improve positional play

ORGANIZATION:
* Field measuring 40 x 25 yards
* 18 players and 4 goals (2 large and 2 small)
* Game of 12v6
* The team of 12 tries to retain possession
* The team of 6 tries to win possession and to score in one of the 4 goals, all within 2 minutes.
* If the team of 6 succeeds, the team of 12 must do 15 press-ups.
* If the team of 6 does not succeed, the 6 players must do 15 press-ups
* Total of 6 series

INSTRUCTIONS:
* Fast transition from defense to attack and vice versa when possession changes
* The team of 12 must ensure that it retains a good shape
* Short passing alternating with crossfield passes

Also Available from Reedswain

Also Available from Reedswain

#149 **Soccer Tactics**
by Massimo Lucchesi
$12.95

#243 **Coaching Team Shape**
by Emilio Cecchini
$12.95

#249 **Coaching the 3-4-3**
by Massimo Lucchesi
$12.95

#256 **The Creative Dribbler**
by Peter Schreiner
$14.95

#265 **Coordination, Agility and Speed
Training for Soccer**
by Peter Schreiner
$14.95

#794 **248 Drills for Attacking Soccer**
by Alessandro del Freo
$14.95

#905 **Soccer Strategies**
by Robyn Jones and Tom Tranter
$12.95

www.reedswain.com or 800-331-5191